Decorating
Candles

Decorating
Candles

Terry Taylor

LARK BOOKS

A Division of Sterling Publishing Co., Inc.
New York

Art Director:
Tom Metcalf

Photography:
Evan Bracken

Production Assistance:
Hannes Charen

Editorial Assistant:
Rain Newcomb

Library of Congress Cataloging -in- Publication Data

Taylor, Terry
    Decorating Candles
        p. cm.
    Includes index
    ISBN 1-57990-243-X
    1. genera crafts; I. Title.

TK4188.R36 2001
747'.92–dc21

CIP
2001029146

10 9 8 7 6 5 4 3 2 1

Published by Lark Books, a division of
Sterling Publishing Co., Inc.
387 Park Avenue South, New York, N.Y. 10016

© 2001, Lark Books

Distributed in Canada by Sterling Publishing,
c/o Canadian Manda Group, One Atlantic Ave., Suite 105
Toronto, Ontario, Canada M6K 3E7

Distributed in the U.K. by Guild of Master Craftsman Publications Ltd., Castle Place,
166 High Street, Lewes, East Sussex, England
BN7 1XU
Tel: (+ 44) 1273 477374, Fax: (+ 44) 1273 478606, Email:
pubs@thegmcgroup.com, Web: www.gmcpublications.com

Distributed in Autralia by Capricorn Link (Australia) Pty Ltd.
P.O.Box 704, Windsor, NSW 2756 Australia

If you have questions or comments about this book, please contact:
Lark Books
50 College St.
Asheville, NC 28801
(828) 253-0467

Printed in USA

ISBN 1-57990-243-X

Table of Contents

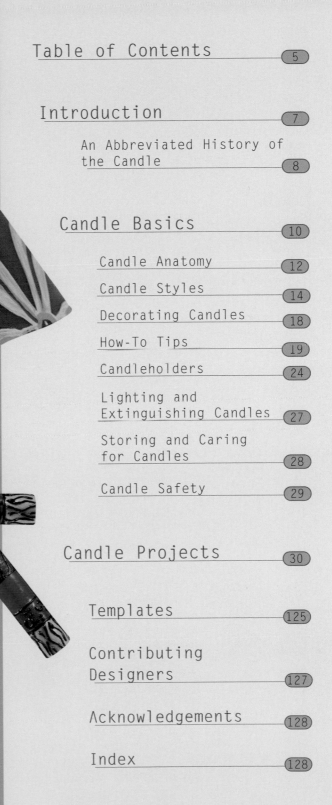

Introduction

Candles aren't the sole source of lighting for our homes anymore: the flick of a switch or twist of a dimmer knob provides any level of light we need for serious work or relaxation. The days of reading Dickens or stitching homilies on samplers by candlelight are long past.

Candles serve a different purpose today. We use candles for celebrations, romantic interludes, devotion and worship, and to brighten our living spaces—even if we never light them. We're presented with a profusion of candle shapes and forms in stores, ready-made to bring into our homes in this year's fashionable colors and scents.

Even with the variety of candles you can find on store shelves, sometimes you just can't find the candle that you really want or need. You might think, "If only that teal-blue candle had a pattern on it," or "Those plain tapers in my simple candlesticks just won't make the table setting as memorable as I want it to be." Or, maybe you want to give someone a very special, one-of-a-kind gift. What to do?

Decorate the candle yourself.

You don't have to make the candle itself, although you can if you really want to. There's a growing resurgence of candlemaking as a craft. Whether they're hand dipped, molded, rolled, or poured into containers, you can make them with readily available materials in your own kitchen. But why bother? Just explore the creative possibilities presented in this book, gather a few materials (many of which you have on hand), and get to work.

We asked several designers to come up with ideas for decorating candles that range from simple, one material, takes-no-time-to-execute tapers to elaborately painted pillars. Create a single, large candle appliquéd with celestial shapes to command the spotlight at annual celebrations, or decorate several small candles to create unforgettable tablescapes. There are ideas for decorating candles for holidays, the family dinner table, a Saturday night with your "sweetie", or "just because".

Use these decorating ideas as guides and, above all, inspiration. Do you like the candles on page 89, but don't want tapers? No problem, decorate a triple-wick pillar using the same technique. The only rules that exist when you decorate candles have to do with common-sense safety concerns, such as whether your materials are flammable. Are we overstating the obvious?

We hope this book inspires you to look at plain candles in new ways: as canvases for creative experiments, lighthearted ways to celebrate, or as quick, easy gifts to create. But don't get carried away and decorate every candle in your house—there's always a need for plain, white plumber's candles to provide reading light when the power lines are down for the night.

An Abbreviated History of the Candle

Firelight was man's earliest source of artificial lighting. It undoubtedly provided the light for prehistoric cave dwellers who painted and engraved the hunters, horses, and bison on cave walls in Lascaux, France. Crude torches that were little more than burning sticks were probably carried deep into the caves, and provided portable lighting where needed. Centuries later, bundles of dried rushes dipped in tallow (melted animal fat) produced a good bit of unpleasantly acrid, black smoke, but were a more satisfactory form of portable lighting. At a later unrecorded date, it's believed that the ancient Romans developed the method of dipping a few threads of lightly twisted flax or braided cotton thread into melted tallow or beeswax—what we commonly think of as a candle.

For centuries, the task of making everyday tallow candles for lighting fell to servants, the housewife, or to professional *chandlers* (candle makers). In medieval England, the members of candle guilds were divided into *wax chandlers* (those who made expensive, beeswax candles) or *tallow chandlers* (the common, everyday candles). In the seventeeth and eighteenth centuries candles were a necessity made, rather than purchased, in most households. A supply of candles was usually made in the autumn, when animals were slaughtered and tallow plentiful, by dipping wicks into a cauldron of boiling tallow over an open fire, or by pouring ladle after ladle of tallow into wooden or pewter molds. It was a laborious and, no doubt, messy and foul-smelling chore. The common tallow candle was the portable light carried from the firelight of common rooms to the dark sleeping or servant quarters of the home. It lengthened the time available for leisurely activities, such as reading, fine needlework, and games of chance, and no doubt lengthened the time available for the more unpleasant household duties as well.

Finer candles made of beeswax were used by the nobility and for religious purposes. These candles didn't produce the smoky flame or noxious odor of common tallow candles when they burned. Conically shaped beeswax candles have been found in the tombs of ancient Egyptian rulers. Around 300 A.D. canonical law of the Roman Catholic Church dictated that candles used in certain rituals must contain not less than 51 percent beeswax. The remaining percentage might have been a vegetable or mineral wax, but not tallow. Judaic law stipulates that candles used for Shabbat must not contain animal fat. Eighteenth-century American housewives mixed bayberry wax with tallow or mixed tallow with gum camphor for finer candles. Candles made of finer materials weren't for everyday use.

The nineteenth century was the dawn of the modern age of candlemaking. Commercially braided wick was introduced in 1825. In 1834, Joseph Morgan introduced a machine with a movable piston that continuously produced molded candles. The first, successful drilling of an oil well in Titusville, Pennsylvania led indirectly to the manufacturing of *paraffin*, which is distilled from residues left after the refining of crude petroleum. This soft, bluish-white wax was a welcome alternative to tallow: it burned cleanly and without odor. Earlier in the 1800s, the manufacture of *stearic acid* or *stearin* (an additive used to harden waxes and make them more opaque) began, and by 1854 it was combined with paraffin to create stronger candles.

Manufactured candles became less expensive and more commonly purchased for use in many homes. By the end of the century, with the widespread use of gas and oil lighting and the invention of the electric light, the unwelcome chore of making candles at home was the exception rather than the rule. By the early part of the twentieth century, making candles at home for everyday use was almost a forgotten art. Candles for special occasions were purchased and rarely made at home.

Today, we make or purchase candles solely for pleasure. There has been a resurgence in making hand-dipped, molded, or rolled candles. We don't need to read by candlclight, but we desire to dine and celebrate by candlelight. The soft glow of candlelight comforts us as it did our ancestors.

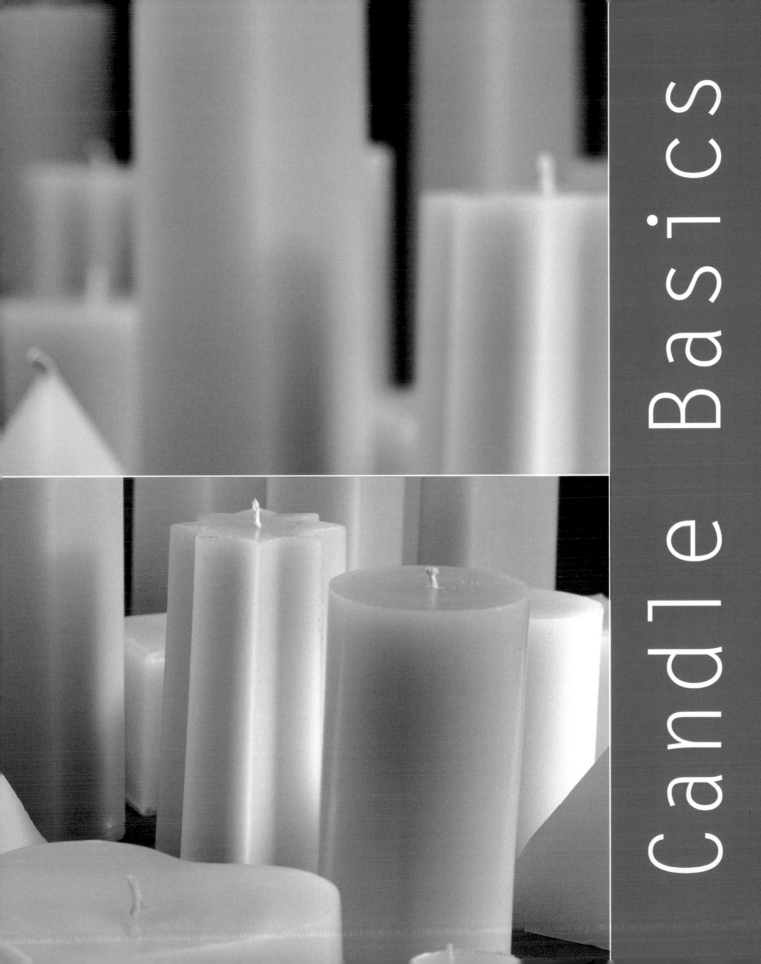

Candle Basics

Candle Anatomy

We learn from childhood rhymes that Jack was nimble and jumped over the candlestick (quickly, I might add). And we're taught that "it's better to light a candle than to curse the darkness." But, do you know that a candle is—according to many dictionaries— "a solid, cylindrical mass of wax with an axially embedded wick that is burned to provide light"?

Well, of course you did, but chances are you wouldn't have described it in those very words and phrases. The two basic properties that make a candle a candle are the wax and the wick. Scent and color are twentieth century additions to the definition, and as for a cylindrical mass of wax, well, just read on.

Wax

Candles can be made from a variety of both natural and man-made materials. Early Chinese and Japanese candles were made from waxes derived from insects (Chinese scale, *Ericerus pela*) or sumac fruits (*Rhus succedanea*) molded into tubes of paper. Modern chemical processes have produced a clear, colorless, semisolid substance for making candles.

Natural candle materials include rendered animal fat (tallow) and beeswax, separated from the honeycomb. Wax skimmed from boiling cinnamon sticks was the basis for temple candles used in

India. Carnauba wax, obtained from the leaves of the carnauba palm, and bayberry wax are two vegetable–based waxes that have been used in candle production. In the eighteenth century, candles were sometimes made from spermaceti, derived from the solidified oil found in the head of sperm whales. Mineral waxes, such as the geologically occurring natural brown type of paraffin called *ozocerite*, have also been used to make candles.

Paraffin, a wax by-product from the refining process of crude oil, is the most common candle-making material for dipped, molded, and container candles. Paraffin is available in various grades for different uses. Microcrystalline waxes, twentieth-century additions to the science of candle making, increase adhesion and opacity, improve gloss, and harden or soften paraffin and other waxes.

A more recent addition to the art and science of candlemaking is a candle composed of processed mineral oils, gelled with copolymers that give it a rubbery texture and clear appearance. In other words, a gel candle.

Wicks

The wick delivers fuel to the flame. There are three standard types of wick: flat braid, square braid, and wire core. They are used in different types of candles and come in a variety of sizes. If it doesn't have a wick, it isn't a candle.

Scents and Dyes

Old-fashioned tallow candles were notoriously smoky and unpleasant to smell when they burned. Imagine the stench of rendering animal fat for tallow, even before the candles were dipped or molded! The addition of scent to candles must have been a welcome discovery.

Scented candles have been made in a variety of ways over the years. Beeswax candles—the candles used by the nobility and religious groups—are naturally sweet smelling when burned. Naturally scented wax, like that from the bayberry, was a welcome addition to homemade tallow candles. Contemporary candle fashion dictates scented candles, available in a nose-boggling profusion of scents, both natural and imagined.

The addition of color—red juice of pokeberries, green from wild nettles and other natural dyestuffs—to melted tallow candles is a relatively recent addition in recorded candle history. The golden glow of natural beeswax needed no coloration. Gilt or silvered paper was often wrapped around candles used in churches in the nineteenth century. Today, chemical dyes give modern candles a variety of colors that change with the season, decorative trends, or whim of the candle maker.

Candle Styles

Visit any candle shop, or your local discount or craft store, and you'll be amazed by the sheer variety of candles being made today. The various shapes, sizes, and the rainbow of colors will delight and possibly confound you. A quick review of candle styles should answer the burning question: "What is that curious shape sitting on the shelf?"

Tapers

Tapers are tall, slim candles, generally wider at the bottom and narrowing toward the tip; they require a candleholder for support. Tapers can be as tiny as the 2-inch (5 cm) tall candles you use on top of a traditional birthday cake to 18 inches (46 cm) tall or taller. Thickness varies from elegantly slim tapers, thinner than a pencil, to the massive beeswax tapers used in large cathedrals. They can be made of paraffin or beeswax; hand dipped or molded; scented or unscented. You can find tapers in solid and shaded colors; straight sided, reeded, or artfully twisted. The ends of tapers can be flat or pegged, dictating the type of candleholder you'll use to display them. In British slang, they're called *tollies*.

Tea Lights

Tea lights are tiny candles, not unlike votives, that are fitted into disposable metal cups. In general they are 1½ inches (3.8 cm) in diameter and a scant ¾ inch (1.9 cm) tall. Originally used to provide heat for chafing dishes or for keeping the tea pot warm, they've been put to a not-so-limited use in modern homes. Usually they're purchased for use in decora-

Votives, heart-shaped and pyramid novelty candles, and a variety of pillar candles—cylindrical, reeded, and flat-sided—illustrate just a small selection of the styles of candles you may choose to decorate.

Pillars

Just as their name implies, *pillar* candles are rigid, freestanding candles, designed to be used on a non-flammable surface or with a suitably sized type of candleholder. They can be slightly larger than votives or as large as the candle maker chooses to create them. They're made by pouring wax into a mold and then unmolded. Today, pillar candles may be cylindrical, square, rectangular, oval, smooth sided, grooved, or textured in many different ways.

tive containers that are transparent or translucent, but we use them in other ways as well: marching across a mantelpiece, nestled carefully in winter greenery, or arrayed on the side of the tub for a soothing, candlelight bubble bath.

Votives

Votive or *vigil candles*, as they are sometimes called, are generally 2 inches (5 cm) tall and about 1½ inches (3.8 cm) wide. They are meant to be placed in containers, usually small glass ones, that contain the melted wax. The term votive or vigil candle is derived from their use as offerings to the gods or saints and symbols of devotion or supplication in places of worship.

Novelty Candles

Novelty or *molded candles* are free-standing shaped candles. Simple pyramids and spheres are just two of the thousands of shapes available. If you can imagine a specific shape, you can certainly find a novelty candle to satisfy your desire. If a mold can be manufactured, a wick and candle wax can be placed in it. You can find shapes that delight the imagination or offend your sense of decorum.

In the mid-twentieth century, small wax holiday figures—turkeys and Pilgrims, bunnies and eggs, skulls, angels and snowmen—were produced and sold in the hundreds of thousands for holiday decorations. They adorned mantels and tabletops in many homes. A jolly, wax Santa Claus candle always stood under or nearby the Christmas tree at my grandparent's house. It just wasn't Christmas until he was carefully taken from storage and placed where I could see him. His legs are now broken and are reinforced with wire; he leans too far forward and his once bright red suit has paled considerably, but he's still lovingly taken out of storage for the holidays. And never lit, I might add.

Container Candles

Container candles are made with a low-melting-point paraffin. Melted wax is poured into any type of container, from translucent glass tumblers to artfully rusted metal containers; antique, porcelain tea cups to terra cotta garden pots. so they do not require any sort of holder.

Gel candles are technically container candles. The clear gel substance that gives them their name is poured solely into transparent containers to showcase the bubbly clarity of the material and any embedded decorative elements.

Decorating Candles

Now that we've surveyed the variety of candle shapes and sizes, it seems as good a time as any to talk about decorating plain candles. Though plain white candles in a silver candelabra look elegant on the dinner table, there's no reason to stop there. Candle manufacturers provide us with candles in every color imaginable. And sometimes, a bit of whimsy or a flight of fancy will urge us to adorn. Our very nature as creative beings sometimes compels us to embellish and adorn even the simplest items.

Tapers are best decorated with simple techniques: painting the surface (see page 98) and wrapping the base are excellent ways to add a special touch to tapers. Because they're thin and burn quickly, be prepared to have extra tapers on hand to replace them before they become unsightly stubs. You need to pay special attention to burning tapers. Read the safety tips on page 29.

The simpler shapes of novelty candles are easy to decorate. Stencil a heart-shaped candle with your beloved's initials, stud a sphere with sequins (see page 124), or paint a pyramid (see page 79). The more complex shapes such as shells, flowers, animals, and the list goes on and on, really don't need additional decoration—their shape is decorative in and of itself. But who's to say that a little judiciously applied paint to the petal edges of a flower-shaped candle wouldn't be a good idea?

Pillar candles are a crafter's delight. The large surfaces are easy to work on. Even painting-impaired people can use a simple decorative technique like stencilling (see page 112). Fond of rubber stamping? On pillar candles it's a quick technique that's almost foolproof (see page 36). Because the wicks are usually surrounded by large areas of wax, you can use more flammable materials that tantalize your candle decorating whims. Pillar candles swathed in tulle, wrapped with thin decorative papers (see page 100), or even wrapped with cloth come to mind, just to name a few. But that doesn't mean you should blithely leave a burning candle unattended! Again, read the safety tips on page 29.

Votives and tea lights aren't usually decorated, but there's no reason why they can't be. Votives are easiest to work with (see page 34) and they make excellent "practice" candles; why ruin the candle you bought in that hard-to-find color and scent by trying out a new technique? Instead, try it on a votive first: if the technique doesn't work for you or suit your particular taste, you can use some other method to adorn that special candle.

How-to Tips for Decorating Candles

Decorating a candle is easy and you already know most of the techniques you'll use. Here are a few tips you may find useful before you start your candle project: measuring and marking your candle; tips on working with wax; ways to adhere materials to candles, and more.

Finding the Circumference of a Candle

If you don't have a simple cloth tape measure, you can use a sheet of paper and this simple process to determine circumference. If your candle looks larger than a standard sheet of paper, use a length of string to measure the candle, or tape two sheets of paper together. You'll need to know how much ribbon (or anything else) is needed to wrap around a candle. You can also use the paper to make a template to arrange embellishments on before you start your candle. You'll find that spacing things on a flat surface is easier to manage than on an upright pillar.

1. Wrap a sheet of paper around the candle.

2. Fold the paper back on itself where it meets the opposite edge of the paper. Fold it up against the edge to butt the edges together. If you need a slight overlap, bring the paper over the edge before you fold it.

3. Unroll the paper and use a ruler to measure from the edge of the sheet to the fold. That's your circumference.

4. Just to be on the safe side, add an extra ¼ inch (6 mm) to the measurement before you cut something. It's easier to snip a bit off, rather than piece a bit on!

5. Once you know the circumference, you'll know the amount of material you need for a specific project.

Marking a Candle

Using a pencil or marker to mark the placement of an appliqué, or to indicate the width of a painted stripe is not always a good idea. Pencils and markers can leave unsightly and permanent lines.

Most of the time, you'll want to mark the candle surface invisibly. Use a straight pin to lightly score the surface of the candle. This is a clever way to mark straight lines, mark the position of an applique, or ensure that a row of sequins is neatly spaced eliminating an unsightly line that could ruin the effect of your embellishment.

Here are some utensils you'll find useful when you're working with wax: a large pot, large cans to create a double-boiler, wax thermometer, and a wooden spoon for stirring. Wax crayons and dye chips can be used to tint colorless paraffin.

Working with Wax

Melting wax directly over a heat source without the proper equipment can be risky business. Don't do it! If you're melting wax, don't leave it unattended. Turn off the heat source if the phone rings or if there's a knock at the door.

If you don't plan to make candles from scratch and just need to melt a small amount of paraffin to cover a dried flower or paper decoration, use the double-boiler method. If you have an old double boiler you're willing to set aside specifically for melting wax, use it. Otherwise, place a metal container—clean, empty tin cans work well—in a pot of water.

When you melt wax to mold into a specific shape or to create a sheet of wax for applique, the wax will melt more quickly if you make wax shavings. Use a paring or table knife to shave wax from a candle or block of wax into the container you have set aside specifically for melting wax.

A durable candy or wax thermometer is a handy tool to have on hand if you want to pour your melted wax at the proper temperature. If you're just melting a bit of paraffin or beeswax to adhere or coat a decoration, it isn't necessary.

How to Overdip Candles

Any size or shape of white candle can be colored with this technique. You'll need to overdip candles if you are making the cut-and-curl candles on page 65.

Be sure to use a dipping container that is deep enough to immerse your candle. If you're not sure whether your dipping container is suitable, fill it halfway with water, hold your candle by the wick, and immerse it. If water overflows, you'll need a larger container for dipping.

What You Need

White candles

Large pot

Dipping containers, large, metal juice cans work well for dipping tapers

Paraffin wax, 140° F (78° C) melting point

Candy or wax thermometer

Wax dyes

Wooden spoon

Oven mitt

1. Fill the large pot half full with water.

2. Set the dipping container in the large pot. Heat the paraffin wax in the dipping container until it reaches 145° to 160 ° F (81° to 89° C).

3. Add dye to color the melted wax until the color you want is obtained. Stir the dye with the wooden spoon.

4. Hold the candle by the wick and dip the candle into the wax for a few seconds. Raise the candle and allow excess wax to drip back into the heated wax. Repeat this process two or three times, or until the candle has taken on the desired color. Let the candle dry.

5. You may add additional layers of contrasting colors if desired.

6. Remove the dipping container from the water-filled pot using an oven mitt to protect your hand.

How to Make a Sheet of Wax or Appliqués

Melt paraffin wax in the top of a double boiler or other container you've set aside for melting wax. Bring the wax temperature up to 145°F (81° C), add the desired dye, and mix well with a clean wooden spoon. Pour the dyed wax into a disposable pie plate or cookie sheet covered with aluminum foil for flat sheets. Pour the melted wax into candy molds for three-dimensional shapes to adhere to candles. Let the wax cool slightly.

Use cookie cutters to cut shapes in the wax sheet when it has solidified but is still warm and malleable. If you want to remove the entire uncut sheet, do it when the sheet is warm. Set it on a sheet of waxed paper or aluminum foil to cool and protect your work surface from accidental dye stains.

Creating Pressed Flowers and Leaves

Pressing leaves and other natural materials is easy to do if you follow a few simple steps. Gather your plant material when it is dry. Try to collect it mid-day, when the morning dew has dried and before evening. Any dampness on your plant material will allow mildew to form, spoiling your pressed specimens.

Pick flower blooms at the peak of freshness when the bloom is fully opened. Choose leaves and blossoms that are well shaped and free of insect damage. Be prepared for changes in the color of your material; it's tricky to predict the final color. As the plant material dries, colors change and darken or, in the case of white, become transparent or brown. Books written specifically about flower drying have more information about the final coloring of dried and pressed flowers.

If you don't have a flower press, use a large heavy book instead. That seldom-used, collegiate dictionary sitting on your bookshelf will be put to good use again. Place plant material between sheets of an absorbent paper such as tissue or blotter paper, make sure that blooms do not overlap. Then slide the sheets between the book pages, and apply additional weight on top of the book.

You'll need to press the plant material for four to six weeks under normal household temperatures. After four weeks, check to see if the material is dry and crisp. If it feels cold or soft, you will need to press the material for a few more days.

When your plant material has dried, use a soft-bristle brush to apply white craft glue to the back of dried plant material. Carefully pick it up, place it on the candle, then gently press it flat against the candle surface with clean fingertips.

Decorating with Flammable Materials

A good rule of thumb is to use a large candle with a central wick or wicks when you want to embellish it with paper, fabric, or dried materials. If you light the candle, it will leave a thick shell of wax around the flame. Thinner tapers can be decorated with paper or fabric, if you apply the materials at the base of the candle. Extinguish the candle before the flame reaches the material.

Don't burn the candle for long periods of time. Extinguish the candle and allow it to cool every two hours just to be on the safe side. Lighting and extinguishing the candle insures that the candle will burn straight down, and keeps the sides of the candle from caving in—a potential fire hazard.

That said, use common sense when you apply flammable material to a candle. Don't wrap the full length of a pair of tapers with decorative rice paper if you intend to burn them. Use a different technique such as painting or gilding.

Adhering Material to Candles

A heat-embossing tool or blow dryer can be used to warm a small surface area on your candle. As the surface is warmed, you will see it begin to liquefy. Press paper or fabric onto the warmed area. As the candle wax cools, it will hold your material. You can also adhere thin sheets of beeswax cut into shapes onto candles using this technique.

Be careful not to hold the tools too closely to the candle surface, or you'll have an unattractive surface to repair. If drips or smears of wax do occur when you're warming a candle, you can shave them off carefully using a craft knife. Then rub the area with a scrap of pantyhose to polish the surface.

Use hot glue to attach three-dimensional objects to your candle. Apply a small amount of glue to the object and gently press it on the candle. Applying the hot glue directly to the candle can result in the candle surface being marred by the hot wax.

White craft glue and acrylic mediums will adhere paper and fabric to candle surfaces. If desired, paint materials with a coat of acrylic medium to match the sheen and luster of the candle surface.

Using Pins and Tacks

Sequin pins, tacks, and decorative studs should be pressed into warmed candle surfaces. Hold the candle between your two hands to warm the surface slightly, then press the pin into the surface slowly and gently. If needed, use a heat-embossing tool to warm the candle surface. Then use steady pressure to press them into the candle. Twisting as you press, like driving a screw, will help. Don't use a hammer to drive them in, unless you want to wind up with a shattered candle!

Painting Candles

Painting or stenciling designs on ordinary white candles is a simple way to dress up a plain candle. The best medium for painting candles is hot, dyed wax, but it's a tedious and messy process. Oil-based paints can be used as well, but by far the easiest

medium to use is acrylic paint. The wide variety of colors and finishes, from primary colors and pastel tones to metallics and pearlized finishes, make painting with acrylics a pleasure. Your brushes and work surfaces clean up easily with water when you use acrylics. And children can use them too, with adult supervision.

Before applying paint to a candle, wipe the surface of the candle with a paper towel moistened with rubbing alcohol. This will clean any greasy residue that could prevent the paint from adhering properly.

If you try to apply acrylic paint directly to the surface of a candle you may find that the paint "crawls" or lifts away from the candle. Not a pretty sight. To prevent this from happening, mix a commercially produced candle-painting medium with your acrylic paint. If you don't have painting medium on hand, you can add a drop of liquid dish detergent to a small amount of paint instead.

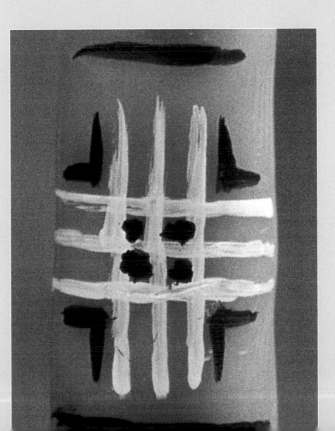

Selecting the Right One

Choosing a candleholder is a matter of taste, and an important part of the overall look you want to achieve. Hand-dipped beeswax tapers are elegant in traditionally-styled silver candlesticks, and rustically informal in hand-thrown pottery ware. A substantial, triple-wick pillar candle on a sturdy metal stand is a clean, modern look; the same candle, surrounded by a circlet of dried flowers and ribbon might be Victorian, rustic country, or another look altogether.

The choice of holders made for candles—from a simple, understated candlestick meant to hold a single taper to an elaborate, multi-branched candelabra—is astounding. Any object can hold a candle, but here are three common-sense rules you should follow when making a selection.

1. The candleholder must hold the candle upright and securely in or on a nonflammable surface.

2. A candleholder should protect surfaces from dripping wax.

3. The candle or candles should never overpower the holder or look top heavy. Not only is it visually unpleasant; the sight of a falling, lit candle is upsetting, as well.

Aside from those rules, anything goes.

Large pillar candles can stand unsupported on a flat surface, but be careful —dyes in the wax of a large-base candle can stain surfaces. Use a simple mat, plate, or some other type of protection. If you don't want the protection to be seen, place your candle on a length of aluminum foil, trace around its base, and trim the foil to size. Large candles with single wicks or large multiwick candles are less likely to drip wax.

Candleholders

You know the old sayings: "When you go shopping for a lamp shade, don't forget the lamp" or "You wouldn't buy a hat without your head." Well, both maxims apply to candles as well. Don't go shopping for a candleholder without the candle.

Container candles, by their very nature, can be placed wherever you want them. Just be sure that the flame doesn't come in contact with curtains or drapes. Also, don't place lit candles on closely spaced shelves or too near a wall. Cleaning the inevitable sooty residue from a smoking candle is not a pleasant job.

An Incomplete Survey of Candleholders

Simple wooden candleholders with spikes, or metal candle cups are at home in either rustic or ethnic-style rooms or outdoors. It's easy to change the appearance of a wooden candleholder to create the look you wish: a simple coat of paint or a more decorative sponge painting works magic. It's also easy to create a simple wooden stand for a candle, or row of candles, with a block of wood and a single nail for each candle.

The simple pottery candlestick, with a broad base to protect surfaces from dripping wax and an applied handle for easy carrying, has been regularly made by potters for centuries. It was used in the most humble, as well as the grandest, homes to carry a candle from one room to the next. Ceramic candleholders often are made to match contemporary and collectable tableware. If you collect a certain style, such as brightly colored and glazed majolica ware, or blue-sprigged Delft ware, or a specific manufacturer, such as Fiesta or Wedgewood, you'll probably find that there are candlesticks in your collection. Use them—that's what they are made for!

The sparkle of glass candleholders softly reflects the glow of candlelight. Handblown or molded;

clear, colored, opaque, or mercury glass, from modern to antique—you can find a glass holder for any kind of candle. A boldly colored glass plate serves as an effective holder for pillars; a small, ruby-glass tumbler shape is the traditional holder for votives; and tapers in clear glass holders are always a welcome addition to any table setting.

Metal is the ideal material for a candlestick: it doesn't burn! It would be difficult to find a home without a single brass candlestick of some shape or size, tucked in a closet or sitting on a table. Silver, silverplate, pewter, copper, aluminum, iron, and gold have all been used to fashion candleholders of different sizes, shapes, and styles. Metal candelabra are more commonly found antiques than ones made of breakable porcelain or china.

Inventory your living spaces: the kitchen cabinets, kid's rooms (if you have them), storeroom or garage. They'll probably yield a hidden candleholder you forgot you had. Dust off the seldom used wedding china, it makes a pretty base for a scented pillar candle; give a toy dump truck a load of votives to carry; little dabs of candle adhesive, a couple of tapers, and that bowling ball that hasn't seen an alley in years...you get the picture. Be imaginative and break the rules.

And then there are chandeliers, sconces, lanterns, menorahs, hurricanes, metal clips for the branches of Christmas trees, and the tiny, plastic rosettes that prevent candle wax from spoiling the icing on your birthday cake. If you're curious, kinara, girandoles, and fairy lamps can all hold candles. Candle snuffers or douters, bobeches, wick trimmers, candle boxes, and bouillottes are specialized accessories for the candle lover who must have it all.

Lighting and Extinguishing Candles

Lighting candles is a graceful and sometimes solemn ritual, whether you're lighting them before guests arrive, just as you sit down to eat a quiet family supper, or for religious observances. Centuries ago in the homes of the ruling classes, candles were lit and extinguished by young servants. It was a simple task for an untrained servant. In the great cathedrals, young men carried candles to the altar in processionals, held candles for the priests to read by, and extinguished them after the mass. One of the prescribed duties for women of the Jewish faith is to light and bless the Shabbat, Sabbath, candles 18 minutes before sunset.

–At the dinner table, light the candles just before everyone is seated. Allow them to burn until everyone has left the table.

Tips for Lighting Candles

–Refrigerated candles burn more evenly and slowly.

–Before your guests arrive, light and extinguish the candles. When you light them again, they'll light quickly and begin to burn evenly.

–Light a candle with a lit candle. If you have many candles to light, this saves you from striking match after match and the irritation of singed fingertips.

–The long-tipped butane lighters used for igniting outdoor grills make candle lighting a breeze.

Tips for Extinguishing Candles

–Hold your finger in front of the candle flame and blow at it. The air will flow around the finger, extinguish the candle evenly, and prevent hot wax from spattering.

–Use a long-handled candle snuffer or douter to put out tapers. The small, conical shape fits down over the candle flame and extinguishes it.

–Cup your hand behind the flame when you blow out a candle. Doing so prevents hot wax from splattering on your furniture or linens.

–A trick for extinguishing tapers for the brave and nimble fingered who don't wish to blow: moisten the tips of your thumb and forefinger, then deftly pinch the wick.

Storing and Caring for Your Candles

When winter's over and it's time to put away the special red tapers trimmed with wax holly leaves, here are a few tips on storing, maintaining, and cleaning candles that may forestall the holiday blues when you unpack and display them next year.

1. Store tapers flat to prevent warping. Place them in a cool, dark, and dry place, away from a heat source. Tuck them in the back of a drawer you're not rummaging through everyday (definitely not the sock drawer).

2. Don't wrap candles with tissue paper. Use wax paper to wrap candles for storage—it won't stick to the candle surface. If the candles have dimensional appliques, loosely wrap them in wax paper, and further protect them with bubble wrap.

3. You'll be sorry if you store candles in an attic, or at the very least, unpleasantly surprised when you unpack them. Temperatures in attics fluctuate widely, and it only takes a day or two of a summer heat wave to seriously damage a candle.

4. Candle colors and any decorative trim will fade if left in strong light for an extended period of time. Don't expose them to direct sunlight or indoor spotlights.

5. If a candle's wick becomes too short to light, use a sharp knife to carve away enough wax to expose fresh wick. Then trim $\frac{1}{4}$ inch (6 mm) of wax off the top of the candle and burn the candle to reshape its appearance.

6. Restore luster to dulled wax surfaces by rubbing the candle with a soft cloth lightly moistened with vegetable oil. If the surface has been painted, test a small area near the base of the candle before cleaning the entire candle.

7. A lightly abrasive fabric—nylon net, chiffon, or even pantyhose—will remove dust and dirt from candle surfaces. Test clean a small area with gentle pressure before you vigorously attack the dust.

8. If your candles have serious stains or blemishes, lightly scrape a knife blade against the wax surface to smooth them. Then use a cloth moistened with mineral spirits to restore sheen to the wax.

Candle Safety

Candle safety is based on common sense, but it never hurts to restate three obvious precautions.

1. *Never leave a burning candle unattended.*

2. *Never place a burning candle near something that can catch fire.*

3. *Keep burning candles out of the reach of toddlers and the wagging tails of man's best friend.*

Displaying and Burning candles

In addition to those basic precautions, here are a few additional tips to keep in mind when you display and burn candles in your home.

Use a specially formulated, non-hardening candle adhesive to secure tapers in the cup of a candleholder. A wobbly candle is worrisome, particularly when it's lit! A pea-size portion on a candle base will prevent your candle from toppling over into something flammable.

Keep candles away from drafts and vents. Even the smallest gust of wind may cause a burning candle to sputter, sending wax onto surrounding surfaces.

Trim wicks to ¼ inch (6 mm) prior to each use. A trimmed wick burns more evenly than an unsightly, partially burned one. A candle that burns evenly is less likely to sputter or send an overflow of hot wax unexpectedly down the side.

Don't burn candles more than four hours at a time.

Moving a lighted candle is never a good idea. Extinguish a candle before you move it from one place to another. Unless, of course, the power is out and you have to navigate up the dark stairs to an even darker hallway.

Extinguish taper or pillar candles when they get within 2 inches (5 cm) of their holders.

Always use containers or holders that are suitable for candle usage. When in doubt, use common sense.

Discontinue use of a container candle when ½ inch (1.3 cm) of wax remains. If you're particularly fond of the container, set it in hot water to loosen and remove the wax, then replace the wax with a votive candle.

Keep matches, wick trimmings, and foreign objects out of the candle wax. Not only are they unsightly, they can catch fire.

Candle Projects

Decoupaged Maple Leaf Candle

Allison Smith

ELEGANT, IVORY SPHERES CELEBRATE THE BEAUTY OF FALLEN LEAVES. IN THE SPRING, USE THIS TECHNIQUE TO DECORATE CANDLES WITH SIMPLE-TO-PRESS PANSIES OR VIOLETS.

What you need

*Pressed leaves**

Ball candle

White craft glue

Small paintbrush

Waxed paper

Paraffin

*Utensils for overdipping candles***

*Read the instructions on pressing natural materials on page 21.

**Instructions and a short list of things you'll need are on page 21.

1. Arrange the dried and pressed maple leaves face down on a short length of waxed paper.

2. Use the brush to paint white craft glue onto a small area of the candle. You should place your leaves on the bottom two-thirds of the candle, well away from the wick. Carefully pick up a leaf and gently press it onto the glued area. Press lightly with your fingers to secure it to the candle. Repeat for each leaf. Allow the glued leaves to dry.

3. Heat the paraffin. Follow the instructions on page 21 for overdipping. Be sure you choose a container big enough to accommodate the size candle you're decorating.

4. Hold the candle by the wick, and carefully dip the candle into the melted paraffin. You only need to cover the glued leaves. Remove it from the paraffin. Hold it over the dipping container for a few seconds to allow the wax to set, then place the candle on a short length of waxed paper to harden.

Tattoo Votives

Megan Kirby

What you need

Any size smooth-surfaced candle

Temporary tatoos that require a water transfer. (Alcohol-based transfers will not adhere to waxed candle surfaces.)

Water

Lint-free cloth, about 6 inches (15 cm) square

TEMPORARY TATTOOS FOR EVERY TASTE ARE IN VOGUE FOR THE FAINT OF HEART. THEY'RE GREAT FOR DECORATING CANDLES WITH SIMPLE GRAPHIC TOUCHES. USE BOLDLY ELEGANT TRIBAL MOTIFS, SINGLE ROSES, OR MOTTOS. FOR THAT TOUCH OF DANGER ON A CANDLE-LIT, SATURDAY-NIGHT RENDEZVOUS, USE BOLD, GOLDEN HARLEY-DAVIDSON WINGS.

1. Cut out the tattoo you have chosen to apply to your candle.

2. Peel off any protective layer as directed.

3. Press the tattoo firmly onto the candle, design face down.

4. Dampen the cloth and hold it against the tattoo for 30 to 45 seconds.

5. Remove the wet cloth and gently peel any protective paper from the candle.

6. Allow the tattoo to dry.

Rubber-Stamp Candles

Jean Tomaso Moore

WHEN YOU NEED A QUICK-AND-EASY DECORATIVE TREATMENT FOR A CANDLE, RUBBER STAMPING WITH BROAD-BASED STAMPS IS ALMOST FOOLPROOF. IT'S EASY ENOUGH FOR KIDS TO TRY, AND PROVIDES ALMOST INSTANT SATISFACTION.

What you need

Square pillar candle

Rubber stamp; a leaf motif is used on this candle

Rubbing alcohol

Paper towels

Acrylic craft paint

Liquid dish detergent

Disposable plate

Foam brush

1. Moisten a paper towel with rubbing alcohol. Wipe the surface of the candle with the towel to remove any greasy residue.

2. Pour a small amount of green craft paint onto the disposable plate. Mix a drop of dish detergent into the paint. This mixture will make the paint adhere to the candle.

3. Decide on the overall design concept and where you will place the stamps.

4. Using the foam brush, apply a thin layer of paint to the rubber stamp. Lay the candle on its side and press the stamp carefully onto the candle. Print additional images as desired. If you want to layer images, allow the first images to dry before you continue. When you have covered one side as desired, allow the stamped images to dry before you turn the candle.

5. Stamp each side of the candle in the same manner, layering the stamped images as you go.

Batik Candles

Diana Light

SE THE TRADITIONAL BATIK TOOL, A *TJANTING*, TO CREATE THE BOLD,

USE THE TRADITIONAL BATIK TOOL, A *TJANTING*, TO CREATE THE BOLD, GEOMETRIC RELIEF DESIGNS ON THESE CANDLES. THIS IS A TIME-CONSUMING PROJECT: IT'S NOT FOR THOSE WHO WANT INSTANT RESULTS, BUT DEFINITELY WORTH THE EFFORT FOR THE GRAPHIC IMPACT.

Tjanting tool

What you need

2 candles in a pale color; use flat sided or column shapes

Newspaper to cover work surfaces

2 flat bristle brushes, 1 inch (2.5 cm) wide; use inexpensive ones—you'll throw them away when you're done.

1/2-inch-wide (1.3 cm) flat bristle brush.

1 pound (454 g) paraffin

Candle dyes in red, blue, yellow, and black*

1/4 pound (115 g) batik wax, beeswax blend

Tjanting tool, medium tip

Tools for melting wax, see page 000

4 clean, empty tin cans

Wide-mouth jar or drinking glass

Hot pad or oven mitt

Waxed paper

Paper towels

Nylon stocking

Nonserrated table knife

*Wax crayons can be substituted for candle dyes.

1. Cover your work surfaces with several layers of newspaper. If you spill some wax, the newspaper will soak it up.

2. Follow the directions on page 20 for melting and coloring wax. Use the double-boiler method: never melt wax directly over a heat source. Melt the paraffin in three separate cans; color them red, blue, and yellow with the candle dyes.

3. Use a 1-inch (2.5 cm) brush to coat a candle with a 1-inch-wide band of blue wax. Let the wax harden on the candle. Re-coat the band to intensify the color, if desired. Balance the candle on the jar and let it dry. Set your brush in the can of blue wax.

4. Paint a 1/2-inch-wide (1.3 cm) band of red wax with the smaller brush. Re-coat the band if needed. Place the brush in the red wax.

5. Paint a 1-inch-wide (2.5 cm) band of yellow wax on the candle. Re-coat, let dry, and place the brush in the melted yellow wax.

6. Continue to alternate blue, red, and yellow stripes along the length of the candle. Remove the cans of wax from the double boiler. Use hot pads to pick them up; they're hot! Set the brushes on several layers of newspaper. Don't try to wash them. If you aren't going to paint stripes on other candles, dispose of the used brushes.

7. Melt the beeswax-blend batik wax in a clean can. Add black dye to color the wax.

8. Spread a length of waxed paper on your work surface. You'll need to practice with the tjanting tool before you work on your candles. The technique is somewhat tricky but worth the effort.

9. Dip the tjanting tool into the black wax. Fill the tool only half full to avoid spilling wax on your work. Use paper towels to wipe the spout and base of the cup before applying it to the waxed paper or your candle. Hold the candle over the can, and let the hot wax in the tool cool somewhat. You can blow on the spout of the tool to cool it as well.

10. Move the tjanting to the waxed paper. Hold it horizontally over the paper and practice making continuous lines and dots. It will take some practice to determine just how hot the wax should be to flow on the surface as you want it to.

11. Move the can of hot wax from the heat source close to your work area. Fill the tjanting as it empties. Move the can of wax back to the hot water to warm it as needed.

12. Practice, practice, practice! Scrape up your practice lines with the knife and remelt them.

13. When you're ready to try the real thing, fill the tjanting with black wax, and draw black lines to separate the blue, red, and yellow stripes on the candles. Use the knife to scrape off mistakes.

14. Embellish the colored bands with dots, squiggly lines, diagonal lines, or commas. You'll get better and better at the decoration as you work up the candle.

Eggshell Mosaic

Jean Tomaso Moore

Pillar candle

6 white eggs (you'll get brighter, truer color with white eggshells)

Your favorite omelet or angel food cake recipe

Paper towels

Newspaper

Ruler

Pencil

Metallic spray craft paint in bronze, copper and silver

Typing paper

Scissors

Disposable plates

White craft glue

Paintbrush

Damp cloth or sponge

If you're fond of walking on eggshells, this is the surface technique for you. Eggshells are usually combined with lacquer for elegant finishes on fine furniture and accessories. Given a new twist, the shell fragments mimic gold and silver mosaic tiles.

1. Break the eggs. Make an omelet or an angel food cake with the yolks and whites. Wash the shells with warm, soapy water, rinse them, and allow them dry on paper towels.

2. Cover your work area with newspaper. Spray two eggshells with one color of the metallic paint. Spray the remaining shells with a second and third color.

3. Measure the height of your candle with the ruler. Divide the height into five equal portions. Measure and cut a strip of paper equal to the height of one portion.

4. Wrap the strip of paper around the base of the candle. Use the pencil to lightly score a line around the candle. Move the strip up and score another line. Repeat this until you reach the top of the candle, creating five horizontal bands.

5. Place two painted eggshells on a disposable plate. Crush the painted eggshells into small pieces. Use a separate plate for each color.

6. Choose a color for the top band. Use the paintbrush to apply glue to a small area at the top of candle. Apply flat-edged pieces of shell onto the top rim of the candle creating an even line. Leave a small space between each piece of shell to imitate the grout in a traditional mosaic. Cover a small section at a time. You'll need to clean your fingers frequently with the damp cloth or sponge.

7. Create an even line at the bottom of the first band with flat edge pieces. When both edges are all completed, fill in the rest of the band with the rest of the eggshell pieces.

8. Cover each band in alternating colors.

Nicole Tuggle

Old World Calligraphy Candles

What you need

Taper candles

Sheet of smooth-surfaced paper for each candle

Pencil

Ruler

Scissors

Books on calligraphy

Dictionaries of foreign languages and phrases

Black writing ink

Calligraphy pen with pointed nib

Paintbrush

White craft glue

Thin rubber bands

Black grosgrain ribbon, ⅜ inch (9.5 mm) wide; you'll need at least 16 inches (40.6 cm)

I'T's THE MEDIUM, NOT THE MESSAGE, THAT MAKES THESE CANDLES APPEALING. HERE'S THE CHANCE YOU'VE BEEN WAITING FOR TO SHOW OFF YOUR PENMANSHIP.

1. Determine the circumference of your candle (see page 19). Measure (include a small amount for overlap) and cut a piece of the smooth-surfaced paper to fit your taper. Make it as tall as you wish. If you plan to burn the taper, you need to make a short covering to wrap around the base of the taper.

2. Visit your local library, or use the vast resources of the Internet to find a text or series of words you wish to copy. It's the elegance of the script that's the visual focus, not necessarily the actual words. You might choose to use text in the alphabet of another language.

3. Use a ruler and pencil to lightly draw parallel guidelines spaced about ½ to ¾ inches (1.3 to 1.9 cm) apart on your paper. Be sure to leave plenty of room in between each line for your writing.

4. Start at the upper left-hand corner—unless you're using foreign script that reads from right to left! Because the nib of the calligraphy pen can only hold a small amount of ink, you'll have to dip it into the ink often as you write. Copy your chosen text using the calligraphy pen and ink. Because the writing is used as a visual element rather than text that needs to be read word for word, it's perfectly acceptable to cut off words. And if you're copying a foreign language, spelling doesn't count.

5. Continue copying until the entire page is covered. Allow the ink to dry for at least 10 minutes. If this your first attempt with a calligraphy pen and ink, wash your fingertips.

6. Turn the paper over. Use the paintbrush to apply a light coat of the white craft glue to the back of the paper. Lay the candle on the

paper and roll the candle, pressing the paper as you work. Use your clean fingertips to press the paper against the candle, smoothing out any bubbles or wrinkles.

7. You may need to apply more glue along the edge where the paper overlaps. Use the thin rubber bands to hold the edge of the paper in place at the top, bottom, and center. Remove the rubber bands when the glue is dry.

8. Measure and cut two lengths of the ribbon to wrap around the candle. Include a small overlap.

9. Apply craft glue to one side of a length of ribbon. Wrap it around the top edge of the paper, pressing as you go. Hold the ribbon in place until the glue dries. Wrap and glue the second piece of ribbon around the bottom edge of the paper.

Quilled Spring Bouquet

Malinda Johnston

CRAFT A BOUQUET OF DELICATE PAPER-FILIGREE FLOWERS USING THE CENTURIES-OLD TECHNIQUE OF QUILLING. THEN, TO SHOW OFF YOUR PROWESS—AND PATIENCE—DISPLAY THE QUILLED BOUQUET ON A PRETTY CANDLE.

What you need

Pillar candle

Quilling paper

⅛-inch-wide (3 mm) quilling paper, in ivory, teal, and 2 shades of blue

⅜-inch-wide (9.5 mm) quilling paper, in ivory, raspberry, and green

⅝-inch-wide (1.6 cm) quilling paper, in pink, and 2 shades of blue

Sharp embroidery scissors

Quilling templates

Quilling tool

Toothpicks

White craft glue

Quilling board, or use a sturdy piece of corrugated board

2 x 4-inch (5.1 x 10.2 cm) piece of ivory-colored paper (or color to match your candle)

Straight pins

Ruler

Pencil

Double-faced tape or hot-glue gun and glue sticks

1. Trace the heart template (see figure 1) and cut it out. Trace and cut out 27 heart shapes using the ⅝-inch-wide (1.6 cm) papers. You'll need three hearts of the same color for each flower you make. Clip a small slit in the pointed end of each heart. Spread a small amount of white craft glue on one side of a slit. Overlap the two edges together slightly to create a cupped shape. Let it dry. Repeat on each heart.

Figure 1

2. Glue three hearts together at the points to make a flower (see figure 2). Let them dry.

Figure 2

3. Make the centers of the heart flowers by measuring and cutting 2-inch (5 cm) lengths of the ⅛-inch-wide (3mm) quilling paper in the colors of your choice. Lightly moisten the end of a length of paper and put it on your index finger. Place your needle tool flat against the paper and press the paper around the tool with your thumb. Hold the tool still and roll the paper around it to form a tight coil. Slip the tool out from the coil, holding the coil between two fingers. Apply a dot of

glue to the end of the coil with a toothpick or the end of your needle tool. Hold the glued coil until it dries between your fingers. Then glue the coil to the center of your flower.

4. Measure and cut eight lengths of the ⅜-inch-wide (9.5 mm) paper in the colors of your choice. Fringe the length of each strip with the scissors. Roll each strip into a coil as you did in step 3. Glue the end of each coil and let dry. Place a coil on your quilling board and spread out the fringes with your fingernail.

5. Trace the leaf template (see figure 3). Transfer the shape and cut 14 leaves out of the ⅜-inch-wide (9.5 mm) paper. Fringe the edges of each leaf with the scissors.

6. Measure and cut 2-inch (5 cm) lengths of the ⅛-inch-wide (3 mm) teal paper; you'll need 32 in all. Roll a tight circle as before. Then, before gluing the loose end, let the coil

relax and expand. Glue the end in place. Pinch one side of the glued circle to form a point. Make 23 additional pinched coils. Cut the remaining uncoiled strips into shorter lengths and glue three pinched coils to the straight lengths (see figure 3).

7. Draw a slender oval measuring 1 x 3-½ inches (2.5 x 8.9 cm) on the ivory paper. Cut it out. Arrange the heart and fringed flowers on the oval as desired (see figure 4). Glue them to the oval. Tuck the fringed leaves around the flowers, and glue them in place. Then glue the pinched coil leaves in place as desired.

8. If you intend to burn the candle, attach the oval to your candle with double-faced tape. You can remove the bouquet easily and save it to use on another candle. Hot glue the bouquet to the candle if you're going to use the candle only as a decorative object.

Figure 3

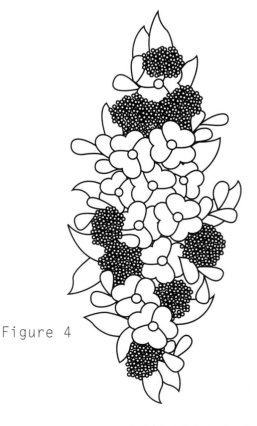

Figure 4

1. Before painting the candle, experiment with the puff paint. Try creating short straight lines, well defined dots, and comma shapes on a sheet of waxed paper. You'll soon discover what kind of shapes you're adept at making. Use those shapes on the top layer of paint that will finish the candle.

2. Lay the candle on your work surface and work on the candle horizontally. Clean the surface of the candle with a paper towel moistened in rubbing alcohol.

3. Select a paint color for the first coat. Make a single line of marks with the puff paint. Leave a bit of space between the marks and rows of marks. Cover as much of the candle surface as you can without turning the candle. Let the first coat dry, turn the candle, and continue with the first coat. Repeat until you have covered the entire candle.

4. Use a second color and make differently shaped marks between the marks and rows of marks you made in step 3. Allow the paint to dry before turning the candle.

5. Using a third color and your most attractive shapes, apply a final coat of puff paint on the candle. Let it dry.

Ellen Zahorec

Impasto Candle

Ellen Zahorec

What you need

Candle

Paper towel

Rubbing alchohol

Dimensional puff paint, 3 or more colors

Waxed paper

Heavily textured with dimensional puff paint, this candle is bright and easy to create. The careful layering of colors makes this candle a standout.

Wrapped Metal Mesh Pillar

Allison Smith

SWATHED IN RICH, BRASS-COLORED SCREEN WIRE, THIS PILLAR CANDLE WILL CAST DELICATE MESH SHADOWS AS IT BURNS.

What you need

Oval-shaped pillar candle

Ruler

Heavy scissors

Brass screen wire, measuring approximately 2 feet (90 cm) square

2 lengths of 14-gauge (1.8 mm) copper wire, each 2 feet (90 cm) long

Pencil or wooden spoon

18-gauge (1.25 mm) copper wire, 12 inches (30 cm) long

Round-nosed pliers

Assortment of large beads (crystal, ceramic, metal, or glass)

*Brass screen wire can be sharp. Wear heavy work gloves when you're folding and creasing the wire screen. If you can't find brass wire, try aluminum screen and steel wire for a silvery look.

1. Follow the instructions for measuring the circumference of your candle (see page 19). Add 6 inches (15.2 cm) to the measurement. Measure and cut the brass screen wire to this length.

2. Measure the height of the candle and triple the measurement. Measure and cut the screen wire to this size.

3. Make a 1/2-inch (1.3 cm) fold on each of the four edges of the brass screen. Crease each fold sharply.

4. Measure and make a 5-inch (12.7 cm) fold along the bottom edge of the screen.

5. Wrap the screen tightly around the candle. Secure the screen with a length of the 14-gauge (1.8 mm) wire. Wind it around the candle a couple of times, then twist the two ends to secure it at the front of the candle.

6. Roll down the top of the screen to create a fat tube. Create loose, random folds in the tube, shaping them gently with your fingers.

7. Wrap the second piece of 14-gauge (1.8 mm) wire around the candle. Twist the two ends together at the front. Wind each wire end around the pencil or the handle of a wooden spoon to create four coils.

8. Slip a length of 18-gauge (1.25 mm) wire behind the copper coils. Twist the wire to secure it. If desired, thread beads on the wire. Use the round-nosed pliers to finish off the ends of the wire and randomly wind the beaded wire in and around the coils.

Country Garden Candle

Allison Smith

What you need

Triple-wick pillar candle

Straight pin

Cloth tape measure

Acrylic candle and soap painting medium

Acrylic paints in the following shades: blue, a light and dark pink, bright green, sage green, yellow, dark red, and antique white*

Disposable plate for mixing paints

#6 and #4 shader brushes

#3 and #1 round brushes

*Mix paint and the candle-painting medium in a ratio of 2 to 1, or follow the manufacturer's instructions.

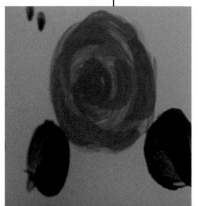

CHEERFUL AND SUNNY BEST DESCRIBE THIS CHARMING COUNTRY LOOK. A BASE OF BLUE GINGHAM, A GARDEN OF ROSES GROWN WITH SIMPLE BRUSH STROKES, AND TINY FLOWERS SPRIGGED WITH TRACES OF YELLOW. HOW DOES YOUR GARDEN GROW?

1. Read the directions on page 19 before you mark your candle. Use the tape measure and straight pin to score several marks ⅝ inch (1.5 cm) up around the base of the candle. Wrap the tape measure around the candle and connect the marks you made. From the line you just marked, measure and score two additional lines spaced ⅝ inch (1.5 cm) apart.

2. Divide the three scored lines with a vertical score every ⅝ inch (1.5 cm) to create a checkerboard pattern.

3. Use the #6 shader brush and blue plum paint to create the checkerboard pattern around the base of the candle. Allow the first coat to dry. Paint an additional coat if desired.

4. Use a #6 brush to paint a ¾-inch-wide (2 cm) yellow stripe at the top of the candle. Allow the stripe to dry and re-coat if desired.

5. Paint small roses using the #4 shader brush to make small, facing crescent shapes with the light pink paint. Allow to dry. Then use the dark pink to make slightly smaller crescents on top of the light pink.

6. Create leaves with teardrop shapes using the #3 round brush and the bright green paint. Allow them to dry. Then shade the leaf shapes using the same brush and the sage green paint.

7. Scatter random clusters of dots between the pink roses. Use blue plum paint and the tip of the #1 round brush to make the dots.

8. Use the point of the #3 round brush to create the small, yellow flowers on the checkerboard pattern. Use the end of the brush handle to make five small dots in a connected circle. Then add a single dot of dark pink in the center. Create leaves using the tip of the #4 shader brush and bright green paint.

9. To make the garland of flowers on the yellow strip, use the #3 round brush and antique white paint. Paint five connected petals for each flower. Use the light pink paint and the #1 round brush to paint smaller petals on top of the white. Add a single dot of dark red in the center of each flower.

10. Create the winding vine on the yellow stripe with bright green paint and the #1 round brush.

Clip-Art Candles

Nicole Tuggle

DELICATE WOODCUTS FROM MEDIEVAL HERBARIUMS CAN GRACE YOUR HOME EVEN IF YOU DON'T HAVE A TRUST FUND. COPYRIGHT-FREE CLIP-ART BOOKS GIVE YOU AN ALMOST UNLIMITED CHOICE OF IMAGES.

1. Determine the circumference of your candle (see page 19). Decide how much of an area you wish to cover on your candle, then measure and cut the sheet of tissue paper to these measurements, plus a small overlap.

2. Make photocopies of the images you wish to use. Use only images that are photocopied—ink-jet printed images won't work with this process. The images used in this project were taken from a selection of medieval woodcuts of herbs. Cut out each photocopied clip-art image you wish to use. Play with the placement of the images you've photocopied before you begin transferring the images.

3. Place an image facedown on the tissue paper. Hold the photocopy in place, and saturate it with transfer solvent. Be sure to cover every part of the image; you should be able to see the image when you apply the solvent. Use a dull table knife blade or the handle to burnish (rub) the solvent-coated image. Burnishing transfers the image. Lift up a corner of the photocopy to see if your transfer is complete. If the image is not fully transferred, you may need to apply more solvent and continue to rub the image with the knife.

4. Repeat this step again, using other clip-art images until you are satisfied with the results. Keep in mind that each image can only be transferred once. You will need a new copy if you wish to reuse the image.

5. Use the paintbrush to apply a thin coat of matte medium over the entire surface of the candle. Carefully roll the tissue paper onto the candle, smoothing out any bubbles or wrinkles with your fingers. Let it dry.

6. Brush a finish coat of matte medium over the tissue paper and allow it to dry.

What you need

Pillar candle

1 sheet of tissue paper, similar in color to the candle

Photocopied, copyright-free clip-art images

Transfer solvent*

Pencil

Ruler

Dull table knife

Scissors

Paintbrush

Matte acrylic medium

*A variety of solvents can be used for the transfer process, ranging from blender pens to acetone to certain types of paint stripper. Choose one that you're comfortable working with. The designer used a blender pen for this project.

Corrugated Paper Candle

Nicole Tuggle

What you need

Large triple-wick pillar

Ruler

Pencil

Craft knife

Corrugated cardboard sheets, in two contrasting colors and types

Hot-glue gun and glue sticks

Drinking glasses, various sizes

Small sheet of poster board

White craft glue

Decorative papers

Waxed paper

Heavy book

Mica

Foreign coin*

Raffia

*Bead stores usually have a selection of oddly shaped foreign coins

As Cecil B. DeMille would shout at the end of a scene: "It's a wrap!" (And the results turn a plain candle into a star attraction.)

1. Follow the directions for finding the circumference of a candle on page 19. Measure and cut one piece of corrugated board to the height and width you need to go around your candle. Since the cardboard is somewhat bulky, don't add any overlap.

2. Measure and cut a second piece of contrasting corrugated board narrower than the first piece and slightly longer.

3. Wrap the corrugated piece you cut in step 1 around the candle and secure it with hot glue. Then wrap and hot glue the second piece onto the first piece.

4. Use a drinking glass as a template to create a circle on the poster board. Draw two or three additional circles of different sizes. Cut out the circles with the craft knife. Coat the circles with white craft glue and cover them with decorative paper. Cover them with waxed paper and a heavy book. Let them dry.

5. Wrap several strands of raffia around the candle. Hot glue the ends to the cardboard. You'll cover the glued ends with a decorative stack of circles you create in the next step.

6. Layer two or more circles together, securing them with hot glue. Glue the coin and a circle of mica to the top layer.

7. Attach the decorative stack of circles to the candle with hot glue.

Sealing Wax Medallions

Terry Burgin

What you need

Candles

Sealing wax

Seal

Hammer (optional)

Waxed paper

Small metal spoon

Votive candle

Ice cube

Wire-edge ribbon

Hot-glue gun and glue sticks

Heat-embossing tool (optional)

Give candles your own personal seal of approval with medallions made of sealing wax. Make several with the recipient's initial for a housewarming present. Don't forget to include the seal and sticks of wax for a gift with special flourish.

1. Spread waxed paper on a flat work surface. Set your seal on an ice cube. A chilled seal will set the hot wax quickly and be less likely to stick.

2. Break off a piece of sealing wax from the stick. You might use the hammer to break the stick into small pieces. Put a bit of the wax in the metal spoon.

3. Light the votive candle. Hold the spoon over the flame, not too closely or the flame will smoke and sputter. Warm the sealing wax until it becomes liquid.

4. Pour the wax onto the waxed paper. Press your seal into the wax. You'll need to experiment with the amount of wax you'll need to make a nicely shaped sealing wax medallion. Make as many medallions as you have candles. And then make a few extra ones just to be on the safe side.

5. Find out how much ribbon you will need to wrap around a candle. See page 19. Cut the lengths of ribbon a bit longer than you actually need, if you are working with wire-edge ribbon. Twist each end of the ribbon. Hot glue one end to the candle and wrap it around. Glue the opposite end.

6. Carefully lift up the edge of a cooled sealing wax medallion. The cooled wax is brittle; that's why you made a few extra ones.

7. Hot glue the medallion to the candle where the ribbon ends meet.

Harlequin Candle

Allison Smith

JAUNTY DIAMONDS OF SILVER LEAF ARE ELEGANT ON A CHOCOLATE BROWN PILLAR. IMITATION GOLD LEAF WOULD LOOK SMASHING ON A FOREST-GREEN CANDLE AND COPPER LEAF WOULD REALLY DRESS UP A YELLOW CANDLE.

What you need

Pillar candle

Sheet of copy paper

Pencil

Calculator (for the mathematically impaired)

Straight pin

Cloth tape measure

Imitation silver leaf

Leafing adhesive

Soft cloth

Soft brush

Antiquing gel

Small paintbrushes

Acrylic varnish

1. Follow the instructions on page 19 to determine the circumference of your candle. On the piece of paper you used to find the circumference, measure the distance in millimeters and divide by seven.* Use this measurement to make equally spaced marks along the top and bottom edges of the paper.

2. Wrap the paper around the candle. Use the straight pin to make small marks along the top and bottom of the candle at the penciled points.

3. Use a cloth tape measure to connect a mark at the top to a mark along the bottom. Then shift the tape one mark over to the right to create a diagonal line. Score this line with the pin. Continue to score diagonal lines around the candle.

4. Follow the process described in step 3, but this time make diagonal marks to the left. This will create the diamond pattern.

5. Use the paintbrush to coat the diamond shapes with the leafing adhesive. Allow the adhesive to dry as directed by the manufacturer.

6. Lift a corner of leaf and transfer it to the candle. Continue around the candle with additional leaves. Use the soft cloth to press the leaf onto the candle surface. The silver leaf will adhere to the areas you have coated with the adhesive. Re-coat any missed areas with adhesive, and apply additional leaf.

7. Apply antiquing gel to the leaf with a paintbrush. Wipe off the gel with a soft cloth. Reapply gel as desired and let dry.

8. Apply a thin coat of acrylic varnish to the silver diamonds and let dry.

* If you want fatter diamonds, divide your measurement by a smaller number. If you want a lot of thin diamonds, divide your measurement by a larger number. Seven might be your lucky number.

Wrought Iron Candle

Lynn Krucke

What you need

Triple-wick pillar candle

Template on page 126

Cellophane tape

Rubbing alcohol

Paper towels

Ball-tipped stylus (or a pencil with a dull point)

Paintbrush

Disposable plate

Candle-painting medium

Burnt umber acrylic paint

Disposable gloves (optional)

Foam brush

Large scrap of fabric

Newspaper

THE DELICATE TRACERY OF OLD NEW ORLEANS' WROUGHT-IRON BALCONIES IS BROUGHT TO MIND BY THIS GRAPHIC INTERPRETATION.

1. Measure the height and circumference of your candle (see page 19). Photocopy and enlarge the design on page 000 to the desired height. Make several photocopies, and trim the patterns to size with the scissors. Tape the copies around the candle to determine the spacing for the pattern.

2. Trace the pattern on the template using the stylus, ball point pen, or pencil. Use light pressure—you don't have to press hard to leave an impression on the candle. Repeat as needed, transferring the pattern around the circumference of candle.Remove the templates.

3. Trace over the impressed lines of your pattern using firmer, even pressure. This time you want to remove wax from the candle surface. Keep the lines as clean and crisp as possible. Use the paintbrush to brush away excess wax as you work.

4. Moisten a paper towel with the rubbing alcohol. Wipe the surface of the candle to remove any greasy residue.

5. Mix the burnt umber paint and candle-painting medium on the disposable plate. Follow the manufacturer's recommendations for the ratio of paint to medium.

6. You may wish to wear disposable gloves for this step. Cover your work surface with newspaper. Use the foam brush to coat the candle with the paint mixture. Use the fabric to remove most of the paint from the surface of the candle, leaving paint in the carved areas. Allow the candle to dry. Repeat this step if you want a darker finish.

Anniversary Candle

Jean Tomaso Moore

THE DESIGNER CREATED A UNIQUE CANDLE TO CELEBRATE A FRIENDS' WEDDING ANNIVERSARY USING A COPY OF A VINTAGE PHOTOGRAPH. YOU COULD CELEBRATE THE ARRIVAL OF A NEW BABY OR SAY FAREWELL TO LONGTIME NEIGHBORS WITH A PHOTO OF THEIR OLD HOME TO TAKE TO THEIR NEW, USING THE SAME TECHNIQUE.

1. Take the black-and-white photograph to a copy shop. Have the copy shop make a color copy of the photo. If you have a color photograph, you can ask to have it copied in a black-and-white mode on the color copier. Enlarge or reduce the entire photo or portion of the image to fit the size of the candle you have selected.

2. Trim the image with scissors, as desired.

3. Mix thin washes with the watercolors on a disposable plate or palette using the small paintbrush. Use the brush to lightly wash selected areas of the photo: skin, clothing, the bouquet. The watercolor washes will mimic a vintage hand-tinted photograph. Allow the watercolor to dry.

4. Place a sheet of waxed paper on your work surface to protect it. Lay the photo face down on the paper. Use the foam brush to apply a thin coat of white craft glue. Pick up the photo and press it onto the candle. Use your fingers to smooth out the photo. Carefully press out any air bubbles and let it dry overnight. Clean the foam brush.

5. Apply one or two coats of decoupage medium to seal the paper image.

6. Lay the candle on its side. Use white craft glue to embellish the bride's gown with white sequins. Cut several tiny pearls from the strand and glue them to the bride's headpiece. Allow the sequins and pearls to dry.

7. Stand the candle upright on the waxed paper. Wind the strand of pearl beads around the candle. Trim the strand to fit the base of the candle. Then, squeeze a bead of white glue around the base of the candle and attach the pearls. Allow the glue to dry thoroughly.

8. Scatter the flower-shaped sequins around the candle, attaching them with the sequin pins.

What you need

Pillar candle

Color copy of a black-and-white wedding photo

Scissors

Small, pointed paint-brush

Watercolor paints in purple, yellow, and red

Disposable plate or palette

Waxed paper

1-inch-wide (2.5 cm) foam brush

White craft glue

Decoupage medium

10 white sequins, 5 mm wide

10 or more white, flower-shaped sequins

10 or more ½-inch (1.3 cm) sequin pins

String of miniature, imitation pearl beads, 12 inches (30.5 cm) in length

Spiked Tapers

Pamela Brown

What you need

Tools for overdipping candles on page 20

3 pounds (1.3 kg) paraffin wax

Wax dye

1/2 to 3/4-inch (1.3 to 1.9 cm) diameter tapers, each 8 inches (20.3 cm) long*

6-inch (15.2 cm) length of wood dowel or pencil

2 cans that are taller than your tapers

Potter's ribbon tool, available in pottery or craft supply stores

Embossing heat tool or blow-dryer

*A pair of hand-dipped tapers with connected wicks are recommended for overdipping.

THE MAXIM "PRACTICE MAKES PERFECT" WAS NEVER TRUER THAN FOR THIS TECHNIQUE. WHEN YOU'VE MASTERED THE TECHNIQUE, THESE DELICATELY CURLED SHOWSTOPPERS WILL IMPRESS YOUR FAMILY AND FRIENDS.

1. Practice the technique in step 3 on a used taper, warmed with an embossing tool or blow dryer, before you proceed to the next step.

2. Follow the instructions on page 21 for overdipping candles. For the first dip, hold the taper in the wax approximately 20 seconds to heat the entire candle. Let the excess drip back into the container, and dip the tapers two or three more times for richer color.

3. Place the dowel on top of the two cans, about 4 inches (10.2 cm) apart. Hang the tapers on the dowel to dry.

4. While the candles are still warm, carefully press the ribbon tool into the hot taper and pull down, making a shallow curl. This will reveal the color(s) beneath the outer layer. Make a curl directly opposite the first curl. Work your way down the length of the candle.

5. If your candles cool too quickly, use the embossing heat tool to warm the area of the candle in the place you want to create a curl.

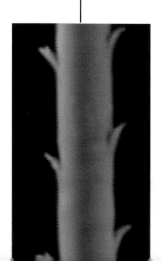

Rickrack Candles

Terry Burgin

What you need

Pillar candles

*Rickrack braid in various colors and sizes**

Ruler

Scissors

Hot-glue gun and glue sticks

*If you find rickrack in an interesting color, buy it. To be honest, it's not the ubiquitous trim it once was on notion counters. Add it to that box of ribbon and trim you're hoarding. Whether you buy jumbo (the largest zigzag) or baby (the tiniest), you'll find a use for it sooner or later.

THE SIMPLE, GRAPHIC CHARM OF RICKRACK IS EITHER MODERN OR RETRO, DEPENDING ON YOUR POINT OF VIEW. IN BRIGHT, PRIMARY COLORS IT'S CHEERFULLY CASUAL. IF YOU USE METALLIC ZIGZAGS ON DARK-COLORED CANDLES, THE EFFECT CAN BE STYLISHLY FESTIVE.

1. Consult the directions on page 19 to determine the circumference of your candle. Be sure you add a little extra to your measurement to overlap.

2. Cut lengths of rickrack to your measurement. If you're using rickrack in a variety of colors and sizes, lay them on a flat surface, and experiment with color and pattern before you attach them to your candle.

3. Put a small amount of hot glue on one end of the rickrack and adhere it to the candle. Glue on additional lengths, spacing them as desired.

4. Bring the opposite end of a length of rickrack around the candle, overlap it, and glue it in place. Glue additional lengths the same way. You'll be able to straighten the lines of rickrack as needed.

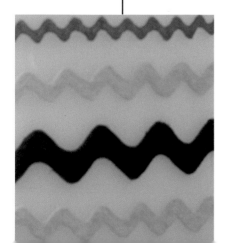

Rolled-Wire Candle Collars

Terry Burgin

Terry Burgin

What you need

Thin pillar candle, 2 inches (6.5 cm) in wide

Kitchen scrub pad*

Scraps of woodblock

Saw (optional)

Finish nails or wire brads

Hammer

*Call it what you will, it's simply a knitted tube of thin wire or bright, plastic thread, rolled onto itself.

Here's an out-of-the-ordinary use for the humble kitchen scrubber. A grouping of several of these candles looks stunning on a porch or deck in the summer.

1. Unroll the scrub pad just a bit. You'll need to discover which direction it unrolls. Some scrub pads have open ends; some are knitted together. This will determine how the knit tube fits around the candle, and if the end will need to be cut for the candle to sit flat. Cut the end of the tube if needed.

2. Gather or cut a variety of scrap woodblocks. Vary the heights of your wood scraps for visual interest.

3. Drive a nail about ½ inch (1.25 cm) into a scrap piece of wood, (just enough to make a hole). Pull out the nail. Tap the head of the nail, point side up, into the hole. The nail becomes the *pricket:* didn't you always wonder what to call that "sharp thing" on a candlestick?

4. Drive prickets into each and every wood block. Set a candle on each pricket.

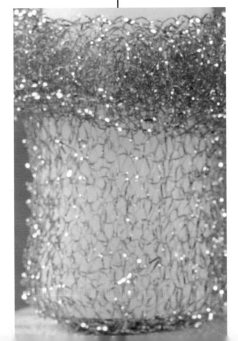

Jean Tomaso Moore

Tooled Copper Medallion Pillar

What you need

Oval pillar, or any type of pillar candle

5 x 5-inch (12.7 x 12.7 cm) sheet of 36-gauge (.2 mm) copper tooling foil

Design template on page 126

Cellophane tape

8 copper-plated nails, ¾ inch (1.9 cm) long

Magazine

Pencil

Embossing tool (an empty ball point pen or dull pencil will work)

Awl or sharp nail

Pliers

Tea light or votive candle

THIS OVAL PILLAR, WITH ITS CELTIC KNOT PATTERN EMBOSSED IN COPPER FOIL, WOULD SIT WELL ON A GOLDEN-OAK STICKLEY TABLE IN AN ARTS-AND-CRAFTS STYLE ROOM, OR IN ANY ROOM YOU CAN IMAGINE.

1. Photocopy or trace the Celtic knot pattern on page 126. Enlarge the pattern if needed to fit your candle.

2. Place the copper foil on a magazine. Center the knot pattern on the foil. Secure the pattern to the foil with the tape.

3. Use the embossing tool with gentle pressure to transfer the outlines of the design onto the copper sheet.

4. When all the outlines of the design are transferred, remove the pattern. Turn the copper foil over and emboss any areas needing further definition.

5. Use the awl or sharp nail to create small holes in each corner of the copper. Then center a small hole on each side of the copper sheet.

6. Center the embossed copper design on the candle. Use two short strips of tape to hold the copper in place.

7. Gently press the tip of the awl into the candle through the holes in the copper. Don't use much pressure—you could split the candle! You only want to create tiny guide holes for the copper nails.

8. Light the tea light or votive candle, hold the head of a copper nail with the pliers, and heat the tip of the nail. Still holding the nail with pliers, push it slowly into the candle. You may need to pull it out and heat it more than once to fully insert it in the candle. Repeat with each nail.

Metallic Doodles

Jean Tomaso Moore

WHIMSICAL DOODLES OF SHIMMERING THREAD AND COILED WIRE SPIRALS SPARKLE DELICATELY ON THE SURFACE OF THIS CANDLE.

What you need

Pillar candle

Metallic sewing or embroidery threads

Scissors

Stainless steel spoon

Tea light or votive candle

26-gauge (.45 mm) copper wire

22-gauge (.71 mm) colored metal craft wire

Wire cutter

1. Cut a dozen or more 4-inch (10.2 cm) lengths of gold and silver metallic thread.

2. Lay the candle on its side. Place a length of metallic thread on the candle. Wind the thread in a spiral pattern. If needed, you can press down on one end of the thread to wind it. Press the thread gently on the candle surface.

3. Light a tea light or votive candle. Warm the bowl of the stainless steel spoon by holding it above the flame; if you create smoke, you're holding the spoon too close to the flame. This will coat the spoon with black soot that will discolor your candle.

4. When the spoon feels warm, lightly press it onto the metallic thread pattern. The thread will be coated with wax and should adhere to the candle.

5. Repeat steps 2 through 4 as many times as you wish to create thread spirals on the candle. You can add very short, straight lengths of metallic thread and adhere them to the candle in the same fashion, if you wish.

6. Use the wire cutters to cut several 4-inch (10.2 cm) lengths of copper and colored wires.

7. Wind the wires into spiral shapes. You may wish to use shorter lengths of wire to make smaller spirals as well. Gently press the wire spirals on the candle surface. You will need to lightly force them to conform to a curved surface.

8. Use a heated spoon, once again, to adhere the spirals to the candle. Smooth out any blobs of wax with the heated spoon as well.

9. Cut short, straight lengths of wire and adhere them to the candle.

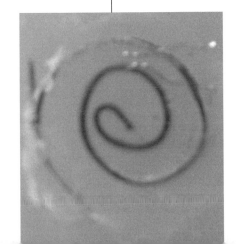

Time-Keeping Candles

Susan Kieffer

What you need

10-inch (25.4 cm) taper or thin pillar candles, you'll need 3 of the same size and type candles

Ruler

Watch, clock, or kitchen timer

Straight pin

Acrylic paint, black and white Candle painting medium

Liner paintbrush

Flat-head studs

Candles burn at a rate that is easily timed. Straight-sided candles burn at a constant rate down the length of the candle; tapers—because they're tapered— burn down quicker at the top, before the burn time becomes constant.

YOUR GUESTS WILL ALWAYS KNOW HOW LONG THEY'VE BEEN CELEBRATING, IF YOU TELL THEM YOU'VE CREATED (AND LIT!) THESE TIME-KEEPING CANDLES. CREATE A PAIR WITH MATCHING OR CONTRASTING DESIGNS. KEEPING AN EYE ON THE THE PASSAGE OF TIME WAS NEVER SO PLEASANT.

1. Light your candle. Let the candle burn for one hour, snuff the candle, and use the ruler to measure the length that was burned in one hour. A straight-sided candle will burn consistently, so you can move to the next step at this point. If you used a tapered candle, relight the candle, time it for another hour, and measure the amount burned in a second hour. Use the second measurement to mark the rest of the candle.

2. Use the straight pin to score marks on the two candles equal to the hour measurements you determined in step 1.

3. Use the flat-head studs to mark the passing of the hours—a single stud for the first, two for the second, and so on. You can use the liner brush and black acrylic paint to add decorative designs around the studs if desired.

4. Mix the candle painting medium with small amounts of the black and white paints according to the manufacturers instructions. Use the liner brush to paint a single line on the scored hour marks. Then paint simple graphic grids to indicate the hours: use single crossed lines for the first hour, double crossed lines for the second. Your design will become quite busy by the fifth or sixth hour!

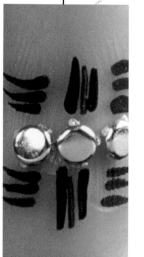

Dreamy Meditation Candles | Jean Tomaso Moore

D O WE HAVE TO SPELL IT OUT FOR YOU? HAPPY
BIRTHDAY...CONGRATULATIONS... WELCOME HOME...I'M
YOURS! CHOOSE YOUR WORDS CAREFULLY.

What you need

Small cube candles

Paper towels

Rubbing alcohol

**Rubber stamp alphabet
and stamp pad, or you
may use letter stencils**

Acrylic paint

Stencil brush (optional)

1. What do you need to say? Count the letters and purchase enough candles to get your message across. The designer of this project spelled out four different words—*dream, peace, sense, and smile*—for a relaxing meditation in the tub. She lettered the candles with one word, let them dry, and then turned each to the right to stamp the next word. That way, you won't give a mixed message.

2. Moisten a paper towel with the rubbing alcohol. Wipe the surface of the candle to remove any greasy residue.

3. You may use a rubber-stamp alphabet and stamp pad to stamp the letters you need on the candles. If you need additional directions, see page 37.

4. If you wish to use letter stencils and acrylic paint, follow the stencilling directions on page 113.

5. If you're comfortable with lettering freehand, use a paintbrush and the acrylic paint to give your message a more personal touch.

Flower Power Pyramid

Jodie Ford

What you need

Pyramid-shaped candle

Rubbing alcohol

Paper towels

Flower template on page 125

Scissors

Dull pencil or ballpoint pen

Small paint-brushes; you'll need a flat brush and a liner brush

Acrylic paints in white, yellow, and blue

Candle-painting medium

Disposable plate

DESIGNER JODIE FORD CHOSE TO USE A DECIDEDLY RETRO PATTERN FOR THIS DEFINITELY DIFFERENT CANDLE. A PILLAR OR SQUARE CANDLE WOULD LOOK JUST AS GROOVY—WITH OR WITHOUT BEADED CURTAINS AND GO-GO BOOTS.

1. Photocopy the flower template on page 125. Trim the template with scissors, leaving a ½-inch (1.3 cm) border all around.

2. Transfer the flower to the candle by tracing directly on the pattern with a dull pencil or ballpoint pen. Don't press hard! You want a faint line impressed on the candle. Wrap the template around corners; let it run off the edges of the candle to create an interesting pattern.

3. Mix the manufacturer's recommended ratio of candle-painting medium with the white acrylic paint. Use the disposable plate as a palette.

4. Use the flat brush to fill in the broad flower petals with the white paint.

5. Outline and highlight the flower petals with the liner brush and yellow paint mixed with medium.

6. Use the end of the brush to create small dots in the center of the flower.

Glamorous Holiday Candles | Terry Burgin

What you need

Pillar candle

Glass-bead strands

Needle-nosed pliers

Paper towel

Thin-gauge wire (optional)

Hot-glue gun and glue sticks

SHORT LENGTHS OF ANTIQUE GLASS-BEAD STRANDS ARE GIVEN NEW LIFE ON THESE HOLIDAY CANDLES. MID-TWENTIETH CENTURY GLASS-BEAD STRANDS ARE MADE OF FRAGILE, SINGLE GLASS BEADS THAT WIND EASILY AROUND LARGE PILLARS. RUMMAGE THROUGH BOXES OF HOLIDAY ORNAMENTS AT FLEA MARKETS AND GARAGE SALES IN JULY; YOU'RE SURE TO FIND A FEW STRANDS.

1. Examine the bead strands. Remove any broken beads from the strand. Use the pliers to crush the broken beads, holding the strand over the paper towel. When you're finished, carefully fold up the paper towel and throw the sharp bits of glass away. Slide the intact beads together along the string.

2. If you're bound and determined to burn the candle this holiday season, skip to step 3. If you wish to use the candle solely for decoration, you may want to re-string the beads on thin-gauge wire. Re-stringing the beads onto wire gives the strand strength and helps keep it in place when you wind it onto the candle.

3. Hot glue the end of the string or wire to the bottom of the candle. This will be hidden when you set the candle on its holder.

4. Wrap the strand up the candle diagonally. If your strands are long enough, you may be able to make several turns around the candle. When you're happy with the way it looks, cut the strand (if needed), and tie it off.

5. Hot glue the last bead near the top of the candle.

6. To store the pillars until the next holiday season, see page 28.

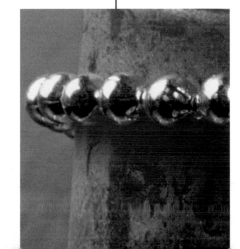

Black-Bearded Wheat Tapers

Terry Burgin

What you need

Taper candles

Straight pin

Masking tape, ⅝ inch (1.6 cm) wide

Scissors

Black-bearded wheat, you'll need 6 to 8 stalks per candle*

Straw braid*

Hot-glue gun and glue sticks

*Craft and floral supply stores have a wealth of dried materials you may substitute for black-bearded wheat and straw braid. Use any one of the many dried grasses they're sure to have in stock. Substitute twisted raffia strands for the braid if needed.

THESE TAPERS ARE AN ELEGANT WAY TO CELEBRATE A BOUNTIFUL HARVEST. WELCOME OTHER SEASONS WITH TINY DRIED ROSES OR FRAGRANT STALKS OF DRIED LAVENDER.

1. Determine the circumference of your candle (see page 19).

2. Place a taper in the candleholder you're going to use. Use the pin to mark the point where the candle comes out of the candleholder cup. Turn the candle and mark a line all around.

3. Decide how tall you want your wheat to be. Then trim the stalks with scissors as desired.

4. Cut a length of masking tape equal to the circumference of your candle. Then cut the tape in half lengthwise.

5. Evenly space the wheat stalks on the masking tape. Lay the second half on top to secure the wheat. Press the tape together.

6. Wrap the tape around the candle, aligning the ends of the wheat with the line you marked in step 2.

7. Hot glue the tape to the candle.

8. Measure and cut a length of straw braid slightly longer than the measurement in step 1.

9. Hot glue the braid to the candle to disguise the masking tape.

Curlicue Icicle Tapers

Terry Burgin

What you need

Tapers

Candleholders

Felt (optional)

Tinsel pipe cleaners

SIMPLE. WHIMSICAL. AN OH-SO-EASY WAY TO ALLOW SIMPLE TAPERS TO GLITTER AND BE GAY ON ANY HOLIDAY TABLE. THE SECRET INGREDIENT IS AN EVER-POPULAR, FUN-TO-FIDDLE-WITH VARIETY OF PIPE CLEANER.

1. Brightly colored felt mats can compliment or contrast the candle colors you've chosen. Craft stores are well stocked with this old, reliable craft material in a rainbow of colors and precut rectangles. Simply round off the corners, quickly snip a row of fringe, or use them as is. The electric blue mats in this project vividly highlight the silver tinsel and apple-green tapers.

2. Hold a tinsel stem between your thumb and forefinger and wind a spiralled curl. Leave about 6 inches (15.2 cm) unwound at the end of each tinsel stem.

3. Wind the straight end of the stem around the top of your taper. Then slide it down to the base. You'd think it might be easier to just wind it around the base, but winding it at the narrower tip puts a little spring in the wire and holds it tightly to the base.

4. Curl and wind as many stems as you have tapers. If you wish, use two or more curled stems on each candle.

Gingko Leaf Embossed Candle

Lynn Krucke

What you need

Pillar candle

Ruler

Scissors

Embossing ink pad

Rubber stamp

Embossing powder, translucent gold

Colored tissue paper

Heat-embossing tool or blow-dryer

Waxed paper

RUBBER STAMP GOLDEN GINGKO LEAVES ON RICHLY COLORED TISSUE. SPRINKLE GOLD POWDER ON THE IMAGES AND EMBOSS THEM WITH HEAT. CHOOSE DIFFERENT COLORED PAPERS AND EMBOSSING POWDERS TO CREATE ENTIRELY DIFFERENT LOOKS. YOU'LL BE PLEASED WITH THE RESULTS.

1. Measure and cut the tissue paper to fit your candle (see page 19), then add a small overlap before you cut the paper.

2. Crush the tissue into a ball in your hand. Unwrap it gently and smooth it out with your hands on your work surface.

3. Ink the rubber stamp with embossing ink. Stamp the image several times on the tissue, spacing it as desired.

4. Sift the embossing powder over the stamped images. Be sure to cover them completely. Create a loose funnel shape with a piece of paper and pour the excess powder back into the container.

5. Use the embossing tool to heat the images. The heat will liquify the powder and create the embossed images. Let the tissue cool before handling it.

6. Hold the candle in your hand and use the heat tool to carefully soften a small vertical section of the candle. Quickly apply the tissue to the candle; it should stick easily. Smooth any large wrinkles in the tissue as you work. If the wax feels very hot, place a small piece of waxed paper between your fingers and the candle. This will protect your fingers and prevent fingerprints from appearing on the surface of the candle.

7. Work your way around the candle, heating small areas, and adhering the tissue. The tissue will absorb some wax from the candle and change colors, making it easy to see where it hasn't adhered.

8. When the entire length of tissue is in place, work your way carefully around the candle again. Heat and press the paper to be sure it has adhered and isn't covered with large wrinkles.

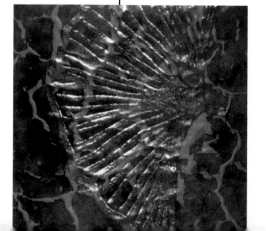

Bottle Cap Candle

Jean Tomaso Moore

WHAT BETTER WAY TO REMEMBER JULY'S LAZY WEEK AT THE BEACH OR A LOST WEEKEND? USE THE TECHNIQUE TO APPLY SMALL SHELLS, FLAT GLASS JEWELS, OR SMALL TRINKETS TO ANY TYPE OF PILLAR CANDLE.

What you need

Pillar candle

60 or so metal beer or soda bottle caps

Sheet of paper

Pencil

Scissors

Blow-dryer

1. Follow the directions on page 19 to create a candle template. Arrange the bottle caps on the template before you embed them in the candle.

2. Use the blow-dryer to soften a small section of the candle starting with the top edge. Push a bottle cap into the softened wax. Repeat the process of softening and embedding caps around the top edge of the candle. Then embed a vertical row from top to bottom, maintaining the spacing of each cap as you remove it from the paper template. Embed the remaining rows of bottle caps.

Jungle Fever Tapers

Allison Smith

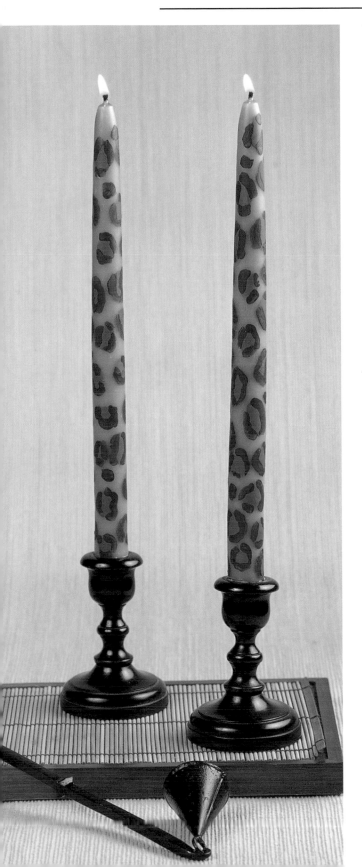

U NLIKE THE LEOPARD, THIS CANDLE CAN CHANGE ITS SPOTS. ZEBRA, TIGER, AND CORAL SNAKE STRIPES ARE JUST AS EASY TO CREATE, IF YOU WANT TO EXPAND YOUR MENAGERIE.

What you need

Beeswax tapers in a golden-honey color

Acrylic candle-painting medium

Acrylic paints, burnt umber and nutmeg-brown

Paint palette or two disposable plates

#7 round brush

#3 round brush

1. Mix a small amount of candle-painting medium with each color of paint. A ratio of one part medium to two parts paint works well.

2. Use the #7 round brush to paint randomly placed circles and ovals with the nutmeg-brown color. Allow the shapes to dry.

3. Use the #3 brush to outline the circles and ovals with the burnt umber color. Use broad, bold strokes—don't be precise—to imitate the appearance of leopard spots.

4. Fill in any large unpainted gaps with dots of burnt umber.

Folk Art Candle

Jodie Ford

Inspired by the brightly painted designs of Pennsylvania Dutch artists, designer Jodie Ford created this cheerful folk art design on a contemporary, navy blue pillar.

1. Wipe the surface of the candle with a paper towel moistened with rubbing alcohol.

2. Photocopy and enlarge the templates on page 125 to fit the size candle you have chosen. Cut out the images, position the templates on the candle and secure them to the candle with a short length of tape.

3. Trace the images with a dull pencil or ballpoint pen, lightly impressing the surface of the candle. Remove the templates after you have traced all the lines.

4. Mix small amounts of acrylic paint with the candle-painting medium on the disposable plate. Follow the manufacturer's recommended ratio of medium to paint.

5. Paint broad areas of color first: the yellow floral motifs, the pink ducks, green stems, and blue vase. Let these areas dry. Give them a second coat of paint if needed.

6. Use a liner brush to paint the accents on the shapes. The tip of the brush handle can be used to create uniformly sized small dots.

What you need

Pillar candle

Rubbing alcohol

Paper towel

Photocopy of template on page 125

Cellophane tape

Dull pencil or ballpoint pen

Acrylic paints, muted shades of blue, pink, yellow, green, red, and white

Candle-painting medium

Small paintbrushes, one flat and one liner brush

Disposable plate

Ladybug, Ladybug Applique

Lynn Krucke

What you need

Pillar candle

Sheets of red and black beeswax*

Cornstarch

Jar or bottle lids, round cookie cutters, or any type of round cutter

Hole punch

Craft knife or scissors

Waxed paper, cut out a 4-inch (10 cm) square

*Beeswax sheets are easily cut with scissors or a craft knife. Dust your cutting tools (scissors, jar lids and hole punch) with cornstarch to prevent them from sticking.

WHO KNOWS WHERE INSPIRATION COMES FROM: WAS IT THE DESIGN ON YOUR COFFEE CUP OR THE CLEVER CANDLEHOLDER YOU FOUND ON SALE? NO MATTER. SO WHEN INSPIRATION STRIKES, TRY THIS EASY TECHNIQUE.

1. Decide what size you'd like to make your ladybugs. Then gather a selection of round jar or bottle lids. The lids from prescription-medicine containers might be a perfect size to start with for a 6-inch-tall (15 cm) pillar. Use coins as templates for very small ladybugs; larger jar lids for giant ladybugs on a triple-wick pillar.

2. Press jar lids directly into the sheet of red beeswax. Use gentle pressure and a twisting motion to punch out the shape. If you use a coin or drawn circle, trace around the shape and cut it out. Vary the sizes of red circles, unless you want all of your ladybugs to be the same size.

3. Use scissors to cut the red circles in half. These will be the wings.

4. Cut circles from the black beeswax in the same sizes you cut from the red wax. Cut each circle into four or more pie-shaped wedges to create the ladybug bodies.

5. Make smaller black circles to use for the head. Cut each circle in half.

6. Use the hole punch to make tiny circles from the black wax. These will be the ladybugs' spots.

7. Place one of the black wedges on the candle, lay the waxed paper on top, and press lightly. The wax paper will prevent fingerprints from marring the beeswax.

8. Place a semi-circle on each side of the wedge for wings, again pressing lightly to secure. Press tiny black spots on the red wings. Add a half circle for the head.

9. If desired, punch out tiny red circles and adhere them randomly to the candle.

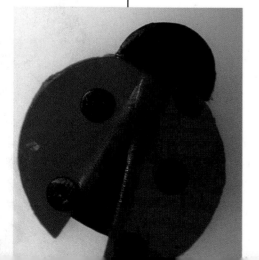

Shell Medallions

Susan Kieffer

What you need

Pillar candles

Seashells, bleached oyster shells work well

Clear glass jewels (optional)

Raffia strands

Hot-glue gun and glue sticks

HERE'S A REMINDER OF THOSE LONG, AIMLESS STROLLS ALONG THE SHORE THAT SOOTHE YOUR SOUL IN JULY. THINK BACK TO THE IDLE HOURS WHEN YOU GATHERED SHELLS AND DRIFTWOOD, ENJOYING THE SOUND OF GENTLY BREAKING SURF AND THE COMFORT OF WARM SUNLIGHT. OR, CALL THE TRAVEL AGENT AND BOOK A FLIGHT RIGHT NOW; YOU MAY NEED TO GATHER MATERIALS.

1. Select shells that have a hole in them.

2. Double a length of raffia, thread it through the hole, and pass the free ends through the loop. Tighten the loop.

3. Hot glue the shell to the candle near the looped raffia.

4. Bring the raffia around the candle, tuck it under the shell, and hot glue it into place. Press the shell into the hot glue as well.

5. Accent the hole of the shell with a clear glass jewel if desired.

6. Additional strands of raffia can be looped onto the strand, circling the candle, if desired.

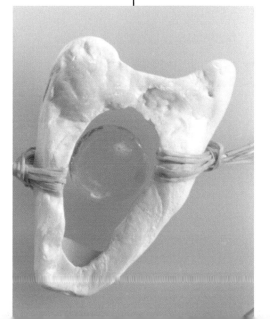

Fleur-de-Lis Candles

Allison Smith

What you need

Pillar candle

2 votive candles or paraffin

Tools for melting wax, see page 20

Disposable plastic spoon

Plastic, fleur-de-lis candy mold

Nonstick vegetable spray

Gold antiquing paste wax

Soft cloth

Antiquing gel

Candle-painting medium

Paintbrush

Natural sea sponge

Small, gold studs

Hot-glue gun and glue sticks

THE REGAL FLEUR-DE-LIS, A CLASSIC DESIGN ELEMENT, MAKES THESE CANDLES FIT FOR A KING'S GRAND SALON—OR YOUR OWN LIVING ROOM. IF THE ROYAL LILY DOESN'T APPEAL TO YOU, MAKE A QUICK SURVEY OF CANDY MOLDS IN THE CAKE DECORATING SECTION OF ANY CRAFT OR COOKWARE STORE, AND YOU'LL FIND SOMETHING TO YOUR LIKING.

1. Follow the directions on page 20 for melting wax. Melt the votives or paraffin.

2. Coat the candy mold with the nonstick vegetable spray.

3. Use the plastic spoon to carefully spoon wax into the candy mold. Take care not to overfill the mold. Allow the wax to cool and harden.

4. Unmold the fleur-de-lis shapes. Squeeze a small amount of gold antiquing paste onto a cloth and gently buff the shapes with color. Let them dry.

5. Mix equal amounts of antiquing gel and candle-painting medium. Paint the candle with this mixture and immediately dab it off with the sponge. Repeat this process until you're satisfied with the appearance of the candle surface.

6. Use the hot-glue gun to attach the molded fleur-de-lis shapes to the sides of the candle.

7. Paint the entire candle with a light coat of undiluted candle-painting medium to seal the surfaces.

8. Center the gold studs between the fleur de lis shapes. Press them into the candle.

Pearlescent Candles

Lynn Krucke

ADD EXTRA GLIMMER, GLOW, AND GLAMOUR TO ANY CANDLE WITH THIS QUICK-AND-EASY SPONGE PAINTING TECHNIQUE.

What you need

Taper candles

Powdered mica pigments, available in a variety of colors

Candle-painting medium

Disposable plate

Small paintbrush

Sea sponge, used for decorative painting effects

1. Pour a small amount of candle-painting medium onto the disposable plate. Use the handle of the small paintbrush to mix the powdered mica pigment with the medium.

2. Moisten the sea sponge with water; squeeze the sponge almost dry. Pat the sponge lightly into the paint mixture. Lightly tap off excess paint onto the plate.

3. Apply the paint mixture to the candle with a light, dabbing motion. Allow the paint to dry. Repeat if desired. Rinse the sponge thoroughly before changing colors.

4. You may apply a second and third color of pigment if desired.

Allison Smith

Oh-So-Faux Leather Candles

What you need

Large square candle

Brown paper grocery bag

Scissors

Work surface covered with newspaper or plastic garbage bag

1-inch-wide (2.5 cm) foam brush

Dark brown or raw umber antiquing gel

Craft glue

Decorative brass upholstery tacks

Blow -dryer

Picture well-worn leather club chairs and a butler at your side with "your usual" cocktail. Cigar smoke is optional.

1. Cut open the sides of the grocery bag. Crush and crumple the bag again and again. The more you crush and crumple, the better it will look. Moisten the bag with water and continue to crumple.

2. While the paper is still wet, smooth it out on the work surface with your hands. Use the foam brush to spread a coat of antiquing gel on the paper. Allow it to dry.

3. Wrap the dry paper around the candle. Trim the paper to a size that's slightly larger than the height of the candle. Fold and crease the edges of the paper to fit the candle.

4. Brush the craft glue onto one side of the candle. Fit the paper on that side and smooth it with your hand. Use your fingers to crease the paper around the corner. Then spread glue on the next side, and wrap the paper around the candle. Smooth the paper as you work on each side. Trim the paper after you wrap it around the last corner to create a neat seam. Allow it to dry.

5. Decide on the placement of the upholstery tacks. If you wish, you can follow the directions on page 000 for creating a template. A template will help you decide how many tacks to use in your pattern and how to space them.

6. Use the blow-dryer to warm one edge of the candle. Gently press the tacks into the warmed candle. Work slowly around the candle, one edge at a time. If you press tacks into unwarmed wax they may crack the candle.

Sculpted Flower Candle

Allison Smith

Forget the sugar and spice—this is a modern, tongue-in-cheek candle for a girl-power birthday at any age!

1. Follow the directions on page 21 for creating sheets of wax. Melt ½ cup (100 g) of the beeswax pellets, and add candle dyes to make thin, cookie-sheet-size pink and green sheets. Make a smaller sheet of blue wax.

2. Melt a small amount of white beeswax. Keep it warm in the utensil you use for melting wax. You will use this to adhere shapes to each other.

3. Use the daisy-shaped cookie cutter to cut 24 pink wax flower shapes. Lift the tip of each shape with the plastic knife to remove them from the sheet. Create the sculpted flower shapes by gently warming the wax in the palm of your hand. Carefully center the eraser end of the pencil on the shape and fold the petals upward. Apply a dot of the melted wax with a cotton swab to the center of a flat shape, and attach the sculpted petals to it. Create 12 flowers with this technique.

4. Use the small end of the #12 icing tip as a cutter and cut out 12 blue wax dots. Adhere the dots to the center of the flowers with a cotton swab dipped in the melted wax.

5. Cut 24 heart shapes from the green wax to use as leaves.

6. Warm two green leaves in the palm of your hand and fold them over the top edge of the candle. Spread a thin layer of hot wax onto the back of each leaf. Set them close together and press them firmly onto the candle. Use hot glue gun to attach the flower shape to the pair of leaves. Create six evenly spaced flowers on the top edge of the candle.

7. Attach evenly spaced flowers and leaves along the bottom edge of the candle. Warm the leaves as you did in the previous step and attach them with melted wax. Adhere the flower shapes with hot glue.

8. Wrap a length of ribbon around the candle. Cut the ribbon to the length needed, and secure it to the candle with hot glue.

What you need

- *Triple-wick pillar candle*
- *White beeswax pellets*
- *Blue, green, and red candle-wax dyes*
- *Utensils for melting wax, see page 20*
- *Cookie sheet*
- *Waxed paper*
- *Small, heart-shaped cookie cutter*
- *Small, daisy-shaped cookie cutter*
- *Disposable plastic knife*
- *Pencil*
- *Cotton swabs*
- *#12 icing tip*
- *Hot-glue gun and glue sticks*
- *Decorative ribbon*

Birch-Bark Candle

Allison Smith

What you need

Triple-wick pillar candle

Birch bark*

Craft or utility knife

Hot-glue gun and glue sticks

Ruler

5yds. (4.5 m) suede strips, ⅛-inch wide (3 mm)

2 or more small rubber bands

Scissors

*Birch bark can be purchased from floral suppliers and craft stores. Never harvest birch bark from a living tree. It will permanently scar or kill the tree.

I F THE WORD RUSTIC CONJURES UP SOMTHING FROM SUMMER CAMP, THINK AGAIN. RUSTIC, IN THIS CASE, IS SLEEK AND SIMPLE—QUIETLY ELEGANT.

1. Use the hot-glue gun to glue birch bark to the candle. Use your hand to hold the sheet of bark in place while the glue hardens. Overlap sheets of bark to completely cover the candle.

2. Use the craft knife to trim the top edge of the bark with the candle top. Neaten the lower edge of the bark in the same way, if needed.

3. Measure and cut three 24-inch (61 cm) lengths of suede. Braid the three strands together and set them aside.

4. Measure and cut 15 pieces of suede, each 4 inches (10 cm) long. Cut one of the strips in half.

5. Gather seven strips evenly around one end of the leather braid. The ends of the strips and braid should be even with each other. Secure the strips with the small rubber band about 1½ inches (3.8 cm) from the end of the braid. Fold the long ends of the strips back over the rubber band and adjust them as needed to create a tassel. Tie one of the short strips around the tassel to secure it. Repeat at the other end with the remaining suede strips.

6. Tie the tasseled braid around the candle. Secure it with small amounts of hot glue if necessary.

Button-and-Bow Flower Garden

**Allison Smith and
Terry Burgin**

What you need

*Triple-wick pillar
candle*

Small pillar candles

*White organza
ribbon, ¼ inch
(6mm) wide, 5 yards
(4.5 m) long*

Scissors

*Small buttons, 20 to
25 in a mixed assort-
ment of four colors*

*Hot-glue gun and
glue sticks*

GIVE ORGANZA RIBBON AND BUTTON FLOWERS AN UNEXPECTED, CONTEMPORARY TWIST BY DISPLAYING THEM ON BRIGHTLY COLORED, HARD-EDGED CANDLES. PLANT A GARDEN OF SEVERAL CANDLES ON A SMALL TRAY—THE MORE, THE MERRIER.

1. Measure and cut a 10-inch (25.4 cm) length of the organza ribbon.

2. Squeeze a small amount of hot glue on the candle. Press the end of the short length of ribbon on the candle. Work quickly, using a figure-eight motion, to form five ribbon petals, each about 1-inch (2.5 cm) long. Use additional glue to secure the loops if needed.

3. Create as many ribbon flowers on the large candle as you wish. Don't place the flowers too near the wick area.

4. Use a small amount of hot glue to attach a button to the center of each ribbon flower. Don't fret about the glue sqeezing up through the holes in each button; it makes an unusual stamen for your ribbon flower.

Moon and Stars Candle

Allison Smith

What you need

Triple-wick candle

Sheet of typing paper

Pencil

Scissors

Craft knife

Small cookie cutters, one crescent moon and one star

Sheets of wax, 1 yellow and 1 orange

Waxed paper

Blow-dryer

Toothpicks or skewers

Hot-glue gun and glue sticks

Vegetable oil (optional)

Soft cloth (optional)

G O AHEAD, GIVE THEM THE MOON AND THE STARS, ALONG WITH THIS CANDLE, TO MAKE THEIR BIRTHDAY WISH UPON.

1. Place the candle on a sheet of paper. Create a circular pattern by tracing with a pencil around the candle. Mark the position of the wicks on the circle you have drawn. Draw a wavy line about 1 inch (2.5 cm) from the outer edge all around the circle. Cut out the pattern.

2. Follow the directions on page 21 for creating sheets of wax. Make a sheet of yellow wax. Place the pattern on the wax and cut out the shape with the craft knife. Mark the position of the wicks with a craft knife. Remove this shape from the sheet and lay it flat on a sheet of waxed paper to cool.

3. Make a sheet of orange wax. Use the cookie cutters to create 15 stars and 15 crescent moons. This will be more than you need: breakage is inevitable, so like a Boy Scout, be prepared. Set the cutout shapes on waxed paper to fully cool and harden.

4. Soften the yellow circle by warming it with the blow-dryer. It takes some time to fully soften, not melt, the wax. Use a craft knife to pierce the softened wax sheet at the points you marked in step 2. Twist the tip of the craft knife as you pierce the wax. These will be the holes for the wicks.

5. Work quickly as the wax shape softens. Carefully place it on top of the candle, matching the placement of the holes to the wicks. Use toothpicks to lift the wicks through the holes. If you feel the wax hardening, warm it with the blow-dryer. Smooth any small splits that occur, and neaten the wax surface close to the wicks. Carefully shape the wavy edges down the side of the candle. Use the blow-dryer to keep the wax supple.

6. Use hot glue to secure the crescent moons to the top of the candle. Glue stars all around the side of the candle. If needed, use the blow-dryer to soften the stars; press them to fit the curved surface.

7. Moisten a soft cloth with vegetable oil, and polish the candle if needed.

Papel Picado Candle

Kathleen Trenchard

What you need

Tissue paper

Photocopy of pattern template on page 000*

Stapler

Craft knife and several sharp blades

Self-healing vinyl-cutting mat or magazine

Sharp scissors (optional)

Hole punch (optional)

Iron

Heat-embossing tool or blow-dryer

Waxed paper

DID YOU CUT OUT SNOWFLAKES AND PAPER-DOLL CHAINS WITH STUBBY SCISSORS WHEN YOU WERE IN GRADE SCHOOL? WELL, YOU'VE GROWN UP AND CAN USE SHARPER TOOLS...SO TRY KATHLEEN TRENCHARD'S TRADITIONAL, MEXICAN *PAPEL PICADO* TECHNIQUE FOR A MORE SOPHISTICATED LOOK.

1. Photocopy the pattern on page 125. Determine the circumference of your candle (see page 125). Test the pattern by fan-folding a length of tissue four times. Adjust the size of your template if needed, make fewer fan folds, or trim the height to fit your candle.

2. Fan-fold the tissue paper four times. Crease the folds sharply with your fingernail.

3. Staple the template to the tissue paper: use a couple of staples in the shaded top and bottom parts of the pattern.

4. Place the stapled tissue on your cutting surface.

5. Fix a sharp blade in the craft knife. Start cutting in the center of the pattern. Cut out the dark heart and drop shapes first. Then cut the diamonds on the folds, followed by the bars that run across the top of the pattern.

6. If you wish, use a hole punch to make the circular holes indicated on the pattern.

7. Use the scissors to trim the scalloped borders at the top and bottom of the pattern.

8. Unfold the tissue and gently smooth it out with your hands.

9. Place the cut tissue between layers of uncut tissue and press it with a hot iron.

10. Warm a small surface area of your candle with the heat embossing tool. Carefully lift one end of the tissue, and lightly press it in place. Smooth any wrinkles with your finger.

11. Work your way around the candle: warm small areas, and press the cut tissue into the candle surface. If the wax feels too hot while you're pressing, place a small piece of waxed paper between your fingers and the candle.

Stenciled Candle

Lynn Krucke

DON'T THINK YOU CAN PAINT? WELL, ANYONE CAN STENCIL. IT'S QUICK AND EASY TO LEARN, EVEN IF YOU HAVEN'T STENCILLED BEFORE. AND THERE'S A WIDE VARIETY OF STENCILS TO CHOOSE FROM TO COMPLEMENT ANY HOME DECOR.

What you need

Rectangular multiwick candle

Rubbing alcohol

Paper towels

Acrylic paints in desired colors

Candle-painting medium

Masking tape

Disposable plate

Stencil

Stencil brushes

Newspaper

1. Moisten a paper towel with rubbing alcohol. Wipe the surface of the candle with the towel to remove any dirt or greasy residue.

2. On the disposable plate, mix each of the selected paint colors with candle-painting medium. Use the manufacturer's recommended ratio of paint to medium.

3. Tape the stencil to one side of the candle.

4. Load the stencil brush with a very small amount of paint, then tap the brush on newspaper to work the paint into the bristles and remove excess paint. You want your brush to be almost dry. The candle surface will not absorb paint. If the brush is too wet, paint will seep under the edges of the stencil and cause your design to smear or appear blurry. Hold your brush perpendicular to the candle; use an up-and-down tapping motion to apply paint. Work from the outer edge to the inside of each individual stencil section. Use additional brushes to apply other colors to the stenciled image. Shade and highlight each section as desired. Allow the design to dry somewhat before removing the stencil.

5. Lift the stencil straight up to remove it. Let the paint dry completely before turning the candle. Stencil the remaining sides, one side at a time, if desired.

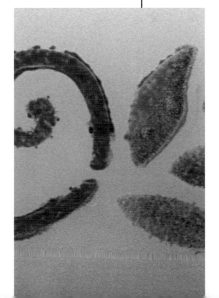

Skeletonized Leaves

Lynn Krucke

What you need

Pillar candle

Skeletonized leaves (available in craft stores)

Waxed Paper

Embossing heat tool or blow dryer

Metal spoon

Craft knife

Small piece of pantyhose or nylon net

NINETEENTH-CENTURY RECIPES FOR CREATING DELICATELY SKELE-TONIZED LEAVES RECOMMEND SOAKING FRESH LEAVES IN A FOUL-SMELLING SOLUTION, TEDIOUSLY POUNDING THE LEAVES WITH A STIFF-BRISTLED BRUSH, AND GENERALLY MAKING A MESS. LUCKY FOR YOU: A QUICK TRIP TO A CRAFT STORE OR FLORAL SUPPLIER WILL PROVIDE YOU WITH A SELECTION OF LACY LEAVES.

1. Select the leaves you wish to use. Decide where they will be placed on the candle. Because they're dried, they won't be able to turn a corner on a square candle or fit on a candle with a small, curved surface.

2. Use the embossing tool to carefully warm the surface of the candle. Apply one of the leaves. Place a piece of waxed paper over the leaf and continue to apply heat. Use the metal spoon to press the leaf into the warmed wax.

3. Avoid applying too much heat, over-melting the wax, or creating drips. If drips or a meltdown does occur, shave the area carefully with the craft knife, then "polish" by rubbing with the scrap of pantyhose or nylon net.

4. Place additional leaves on the candle as desired.

Oriental Candles

Jean Tomaso
Moore and
Susan Kieffer

SIMILAR MATERIALS AND TECHNIQUES CAN CREATE DIFFERENT LOOKS ON SIMILAR TYPES OF CANDLES. THE BAMBOO CANDLE JEAN CREATED (ON RIGHT) NEEDS A FEW HAND TOOLS TO MAKE. SUSAN'S GREENER, DRIED MATERIAL, AN EQUISETUM, CAN BE CUT WITH SCISSORS. THE RESULTS ARE EQUALLY STUNNING.

What you need

Pillar candle

Ruler

½-inch (1.3 cm) diameter bamboo stalks*

Handsaw

Small chisel

Hammer

Rubber band

Scissors

Blow-dryer

Raffia strands

Glass beads (optional)

12-inch (30.5 cm) length of 22-gauge wire

Wire cutter

*Use bamboo plant stakes found in a garden center or dried stalks of Equisetum from a florist or craft store.

1. Measure the height of your candle. Cut six lengths of the bamboo to the needed height with the handsaw. If you've chosen to cover a very large candle, you may need additional lengths.

2. Lay a single cut length of bamboo on its side (diameter) against a worktable, and center the chisel on the diameter of the bamboo. Using the chisel as a wedge, lightly tap the hammer onto the chisel. The bamboo will split down the center. Split all cut pieces in this fashion.

3. Place two split bamboo pieces (cut side facing in) on the candle. Use the rubber band to hold them in place. Then slip additional lengths of bamboo under the rubber band, and cover the entire surface of the candle. You can space the bamboo close together or use wider spacing to allow the color and pattern of your candle to shine through. Remove the rubber bands.

4. Use the blow dryer to slowly soften the wax on a small area of the candle. Push a length of bamboo into the softened wax. Work around the entire candle.

5. Wrap a length of wire around the bamboo. Twist the ends together tightly and trim close to the wire.

6. Wind several strands of raffia around the candle to disguise the wire.

7. Thread the glass beads on single strands of raffia. Knot the end of the strands to hold the beads in place.

Homage to Mondrian Candle

Jodie Ford

What you need

Flat-sided white candle

Rubbing alcohol

Paper towel

Ruler

Sewing needle or straight pin

Small paint-brushes, you'll need a flat brush and a liner brush

Acrylic paints, you'll need red, blue, yellow, and black

Candle-painting medium

Disposable plate to mix paints on

A SIMPLE CUBE-SHAPED CANDLE IS THE PERFECT CANVAS TO BRUSH UP ON MODERN ART HISTORY. START WITH THE GEOMETRIC STYLE OF PIET MONDRIAN. THEN MOVE ON TO WATERLILIES IN THE STYLE OF MONET, OR PERHAPS SOMETHING FROM YOUR BLUE PERIOD.

1. Clean the surface of the candle with a paper towel moistened with rubbing alcohol.

2. Lay the candle flat on your work surface. Use the ruler and the needle or pin to lightly score irregularly spaced horizontal and vertical lines on the candle's surface. The vertical and horizontal lines will create small square and rectangular shapes. Score the remaining three sides of the candle.

3. Mix a small amount of acrylic paint with the manufacturer's recommended amount of candle-painting medium. Use a small, flat brush to paint several shapes on one side of the candle. Let them dry. Turn the candle and paint several shapes on the next side. Repeat until you have used one color on each of the four sides.

4. Mix a small amount of a second color and repeat step 2.

5. Mix a small amount of your third color. Paint some shapes in this color, but leave some shapes unpainted.

6. Use the liner brush to outline all of the shapes with black paint.

Beaded Candle Rings

Jean Tomaso Moore

THESE SIMPLY MADE AND VERSATILE BEADED RINGS WILL DRESS UP ANY CANDLE. THEY'RE EASILY REMOVED AS THE CANDLE BURNS DOWN AND YOUR CANDLE DECORATION— UNLIKE OTHERS—IS READY TO USE AGAIN!

What you need

Reeded taper candles, or any cylindrical candle

26-gauge (.45 mm) copper wire, 5 yards (4.5 m) in length

Selection of glass seed beads, bugle beads, and semi-precious stone beads

Wire cutters

Round-nose pliers (optional)

1. Follow the instructions on page 19 to determine the circumference of your candle. Use the wire cutters to cut a length of copper wire measuring 2 inches (5.1 cm) longer than the circumference of the candle. Cut nine more lengths of wire, and set them aside.

2. Make a loosely tied knot at one end of a length of wire. The gauge of the wire is fine enough to knot.

3. Thread beads onto the wire. Vary the placement of bead color, texture, and size for interest. Thread just enough beads onto the wire to wrap around the candle. Wind the beaded wire around the candle and check for fit. You may need to add or subtract beads.

4. Pull the unbeaded end through the loosely formed knot, forming a ring. The ring should be snug enough to sit on the candle without sliding down.

5. When you're satisfied with the fit, slide the beaded ring off the candle, and wind the remaining tail of wire around the ring. Hide the wire in place between the beads.

6. Make as many rings as desired, following steps 2 through 5. You can make them all identical or vary the placement of the beads.

7. You can space the rings all along the height, or settle them near the base of the candle. As the candle burns down, the ring closest to the wick can be slipped off and used on another candle.

Midnight Safari Candles

Diana Light

Diana Light

What you need

Taper candles

Animal print fabric, 3 x 6 inches (7.6 x 15.2 cm) in length

Black ribbon, 12 inches (30.5 cm) long

Gold-colored seed beads

Beading needle

Black bead thread

Scissors

Hot-glue gun and glue sticks

SWATCHES OF FABRIC AND FANCIFUL NOTIONS ARE JUST ABOUT THE ONLY THINGS YOU NEED TO QUICKLY ADD AN IMAGINATIVE SPARK TO PLAIN, BORING TAPER CANDLES. LEOPARD PRINT, EDGED IN TINY GOLD BEADS ON BLACK RIBBON, ADORNING SHOCKING RED CANDLES, SUGGESTS DANGER AHEAD.

1. Measure the circumference of your candle (see page 19). Add ¼ inch (6 mm) to this measurement. Measure and cut four lengths of the black ribbon to size.

2. Thread the beading needle and knot one end of the thread. Stitch the gold seed beads to one edge of each length of ribbon, spacing them about ¼ inch (6 mm) apart.

3. Measure and cut two lengths of the fabric to fit your candles. Attach the fabric to both candles with hot glue.

4. Position a length of ribbon so that it overlaps the edge of the fabric just enough to hide the cut edge. Attach it to the candle with hot glue. Repeat with the bottom edge of the fabric. Conceal the edges of the fabric on the second candle as well.

Variations

Rummage through your fabric and trim stash (or a friend's): everyone has one, even if they deny it! You'll discover a wealth of materials for quick candle dress-ups. Feeling demure? A scrap of lace edged with tiny pearls on a pale blue candle may be just what you desire. Curl a bit of wire mesh on a pencil for a contemporary take on an Ionic capital. Upholstery trims or ribbons, chenille stems or short lengths of wire, can be glued on or simply wrapped and tied.

Sequinned Sphere

Jean Tomaso Moore

What You Need

Ball candle

Bottle cap

Straight pin

8mm black sequins

8mm white sequins

1/2-inch (1.3 cm) sequin pins

Leather finger thimble (optional)

As GRAPHICALLY ELEGANT AS WHITE-TIE AND TAILS, THIS SEQUIN-STUDDED CANDLE WOULD HAVE MADE FRED AND GINGER SMILE.

1. Center the bottle cap over the wick. Use the straight pin to score a light outline of the cap on the candle. All sequins will be placed outside of this circle. If you plan to burn the candle, make the circle just a bit larger to create a buffer zone for melted wax as the candle burns.

2. Use sequin pins to secure the sequins to the candle. You'll find it helpful, and less painful, to wear the leather thimble when you push the pins into the candle.

3. Work from the top of the candle down to the base. Start with a single row of white sequins. Overlap the sequins slightly, and follow the curve of the candle. Then add two rows of black sequins in the same way.

4. Alternate double rows of black and white until you are pleased with the overall design.

5. Finish the pattern with a single row of white sequins.

Papel Picado Template

(page 110)

Flower Power Template

(page 78)

Folk Art Templates

(page 91)

Wrought Iron Template

(page 60)

Tooled Copper Template

(page 70)

Contributing Designers

Pamela Brown owns a specialty lighting and candle shop, Mountain Lights, in downtown Asheville, North Carolina. She teaches candlemaking classes in her shop, and at John C. Campbell Folk School, in Brasstown, North Carolina.

Terry Burgin is an artist, craft designer, and the author of this book. He's never met a craft (yet!) that he wouldn't try, given the chance.

Jodi Ford is a graduate of The Savannah College of Art and Design. She's a freelance designer living in Asheville, North Carolina.

Malinda Johnston is the author of *Paper Quilling* (Lark, 1998) and the owner of Lake City Craft Company in Nixa, Missouri. Visit her Website at: www.lakecitycraft.com.

Susan Kieffer traded the sand, sun, and fun of Key West for the Blue Ridge mountains of Asheville, North Carolina. Her resume runs the gamut from catalog buyer to television camerawoman to clothing designer. She works for *Folkwear Patterns* and *Fiberarts*.

Megan Kirby is a graphic designer for *Fiberarts*. She lives in Asheville, North Carolina.

Diana Light is an artisan, designer, and co-author of *Etching Glass (Lark, 2000)*. She sells her work through her Blue Light Boutique in Weaverville, North Carolina. Visit the boutique's Website at: www.angelfire.com/NC2/diana/bluelight.html.

Jean Tomaso Moore has been creating art in one form or another for as long as she can remember. She lives with her humble, patient husband, Richard, in the beautiful mountains of Asheville, North Carolina.

Allison Smith juggles motherhood, craft design, and her home-based business in Asheville, North Carolina. Her business specializies in providing deluxe tourist accommodations worldwide. You can reach her via e-mail at: waterrock-garden@hotmail.com.

Kathleen Trenchard is the author of *Mexican Papercutting* (Lark, 1998) and the owner of Cut-It-Out in San Antonio, Texas. You can view her work on the Internet at: www.web-net.com/cut-it-out.

Nicole Tuggle combines bookbinding techniques with her passion for mail art to create unique letters, fine art, and gift items. Visit her Website at: www.sigilation.com.

Ellen Zahorec has exhibited her mixed media work nationally and internationally. She is the owner of Zahorec-Hughes Gallery in Cincinnati, Ohio.

Acknowledgments

Finding the perfect candleholder for each candle project would not have been possible without generous loans from the following Asheville, North Carolina businesses and individuals: Flowers on Broadway, The L.O.F.T. , Mountain Lights, The Natural Home, Pier One, Stuff Antiques; Miegan Gordon, Susan Kieffer, Faye Taylor, and Wade Bryant. Special thanks to the talented folks at Guinivere's for creating the candles shown on pages 14-16.

Index